Chronically Ill,

Wildly Capable!

Chronically Ill, *Wildly Capable!*

How to Build A Flexible Career,
Protect Your Energy,
and Create Sustainable Success

KRISTINA KELLY

ISBN 979-8-9924917-2-2 (paperback)

ISBN 979-8-9924917-3-9 (e-book)

Also by Kristina Kelly

**How to Be a Badass in a
Broken Healthcare System**

*Overlooked to Empowered:
A Guide for Chronically Ill Patients
Who Refuse to Settle*

Dedication

To B, because I know it was damn uncomfortable to support my out-of-the-box dreams sometimes, but you always did. Thank you for believing in me.

Contents

Introduction

This book did not go according to plan. Many years ago, I had a grand idea to write a book called *Wishes Are for Wussies: How to Have Success Without Luck, Chance, or Circumstance.* Catchy title, eh? It was going to be the ultimate "stop whining and start winning" guide for people stuck in jobs they couldn't stand and too terrified to leave for something better. I had 30,000 tough-love words in the works, a clear vision, and a slightly unhealthy amount of caffeine coursing through my body.

You see, I was a chronic job-hopper before I found success on my own terms. I had fourteen jobs in twenty-five years!

Now, hear me out before you ask, "Why should I take job advice from this chick?"

I'll tell you why. I had endured jobs that made me cry in the parking lot. Dealt with work bullies who were seriously stuck in a middle school mentality. I learned what I hated, what I could tolerate, and what I actually enjoyed. Eventually, I figured out that the problem wasn't me (ok, sometimes it *was* me)—it was the outdated idea that success only comes from following the traditional career ladder. So, I built my own damn ladder. I left the corporate world to start my own business. And it worked! More on how I did it later. I had a thriving digital marketing business, I was making more money than ever, and I was living proof that you didn't need luck or some cosmic alignment of the stars to succeed. I was ready to package that knowledge into a book and teach people how to take control of their careers, just as I had.

But then I got sick.

I stopped writing the book, but at first, I didn't know why. Maybe I had imposter syndrome? That didn't feel quite right. Writer's block? But I was on such a roll. Then I realized it was the phantom prankster that hijacked my immune system. My health became an all-consuming mystery, leading me down a nightmarish rabbit hole of misdiagnoses, medical gaslighting, and waiting rooms that smelled like despair and antibacterial gel.

The book gathered dust on the shelf while I focused on surviving.

If you've read my first book, *How to Be a Badass in a Broken Healthcare System*, you already know what happened next. I fought like hell for answers. Eventually, the medical community admitted that, yes, something was indeed wrong with me. Sjogren's disease, seronegative myasthenia gravis, non-radiographic axial spondyloarthritis, and a collection of their freeloading sidekicks had become my real-life roommates—and I couldn't evict them. The hustle-until-you-make-it mindset that built my career now felt downright toxic.

So, what happens when the very strategies that got you where you are become nearly worthless? When ambition is no longer enough? When your body refuses to cooperate with your career goals, but you still have bills to pay, responsibilities to meet, and some shred of personal identity to maintain?

I had to rethink everything. No more taking every client who wanted to work with me. My energy was now a finite resource, and I needed to spend my time wisely. I had to screen potential clients as much as they screened me. Could I handle their workload without setting my health on fire? Were they going to stress me out so badly that my symptoms would flare within a week? Would they expect 24/7 availability when I could barely commit to 6/5? If the answer was yes, I had to say no. And let me tell you, saying no when you've been conditioned to say yes is as uncomfortable as a wool thong on a hot summer day.

I worried I wouldn't be able to pay my bills. I worried I'd have to go back to corporate life, commuting, sitting in an office chair for eight hours a day, pretending I wasn't contemplating taking a nap in the bathroom stall. I worried my career (the one I had built from nothing) was over.

But guess what? I figured it out.

I maintained my income while working only 25-30 hours a week. I let go of the traditional definition of a singular dream job and created a portfolio of *jobs* that worked for me. I'm a part-time digital marketing freelancer, part-time board certified patient advocate, and author when I have the spoons for it. There were years when I was so sick I could barely work ten hours a week, but as I slowly started to regain some energy and reduce my symptoms, I managed to set sail on a new course.

I know there are people out there who can't even manage ten hours a week. And if that's you, I need you to know this:

I see you. I believe you. Maybe you're reading this book for inspiration, storing away ideas for when you're feeling a little better. Maybe you're managing your disease well enough to start making changes, but you just don't know where to start. Maybe you're somewhere in between, wondering if success is even possible for someone in your body.

Wherever you are in your career journey, my goal is to provide you with practical tools to build a career on your terms that doesn't require grinding yourself into dust to feel valuable. You are valuable just the way you are. Your job should fit your life, not the other way around.

Once I got sick, the entire concept of "not wishing for change" from my original book idea lost its appeal. I think it's a big reason why I let this book sit on a shelf for so long. The concept of "hustling until you make it" is part of the productivity culture that I no longer aligned myself with. I could no longer push through at all costs.

Wishes are now replaced with intention. I know when to adapt, when to pivot, and when to redefine what success actually looks like. Chronic illness is an unfair wildcard that forces you to rewrite the rules of life.

And that's precisely what this book will help you do.

One last thing before we dive in. Depression, anxiety, and every emotion that floats in between are real and deserve to be taken seriously. I've seen firsthand what it looks like when you want to play the game of life, but your mind and body won't get off the bench. If you're struggling, please ask for help from a mental health professional. If even making the appointment feels overwhelming, please ask someone—your partner, a friend, a neighbor, or someone at church—to book it for you.

Now, let's get to work (in a slow, comfortable manner). We're going to ditch the wish, redefine success, and figure out how to be a badass in a broken work world.

What You'll Learn

If I haven't made it clear yet, this is not a book about traditional job advice. It isn't about powering through or ignoring your body. It's about building a custom career that works for you. In this book you'll learn how to:

- Redefine success when the traditional career path isn't an option.
- Pivot and adapt when your health throws curveballs.
- Budget your energy and work smarter, not harder.
- Manage remote jobs, freelancing, gigs, and career paths that align more with chronic illness.
- Advocate for accommodations without fear.
- Survive career setbacks and financial instability.
- Kick imposter syndrome and work guilt to the curb.
- Create a career that evolves with your health.

At first glance, it may feel overwhelming. I recall how swamped I felt when I pivoted my career while I was healthy! It's a whole new ballpark now, so I get it. Please remember this is like the turtle running the race. The rabbit is the career we are leaving behind. The turtle is still the winner— just on his schedule. I want you to work at your pace.

How This Book Is Structured

At the end of every chapter, you'll find a Work-Life Playbook that lists Résumé Highlights (Key Lessons from the Chapter), Power Moves (Actionable Steps to Apply What You've Learned), and CEO Mindset Check-In (Reflective Questions to Apply to Your Own Career). You can grab a journal or note app to jot your thoughts and learnings that really stick out to you. This book is packed with a ton of information, so you can use the Work-Life Playbook at the end of each chapter when you need a refresher, extra motivation, or renewed guidance.

Alright, my fellow work-from-bed warrior, grab your happy drink of choice, a healthy snack, your favorite loungewear, and let's start laying the foundation for this new, fabulous chapter of your career!

Chapter 1

Redefine Success & Ditch the Traditional Definition of Your "Dream Job"

A dream career may sound impossible when you're stuck fantasizing about something as basic as finally getting a diagnosis or a treatment that works. Or even dreaming about having the energy to take a shower without feeling like your soul gets liquefied and poured down the drain. I'll be the first to admit that when survival is on the line, the phrase "dream career" feels a bit like toxic positivity.

Success doesn't always look like the version you imagined in your youth. Back then, it felt easy to believe life would move in a straight line, with goals checked off in order, and everything clicking into place. By now you have learned that life rarely plays out that neat and tidy. So, we're swapping a dream career for adaptive ambition!

I once read a book called *A Cancer Warrior: How I Fought and Survived My Battle With Pancreatic Cancer,* by Dusty Mason. I picked it up for a family member who was deep in the trenches of their battle with pancreatic cancer. I hoped to learn how Mason had beaten the odds. The title grabbed me, especially those two words: fought and survived. Past tense. It made me think, "This guy must have figured it out. He must have won."

As I read through the book, I kept anticipating the exact moment the author would reveal how he cured himself. But after I finished reading the last page, I realized Mason had not "beaten" cancer the way I envisioned. Yes, he was a warrior with a fighting spirit that I could hardly fathom and entirely respected. But he had not discovered a magic sauce. He had not found a unique type of therapy that no one else was aware of. Pancreatic cancer has a devastatingly high recurrence rate, meaning it could come back at any time.

I don't want to say I felt cheated, but I felt a little misled.

However, something prompted me to revisit the last chapter, and in doing so, it completely reframed my understanding of his journey. The author explained that his definition of "beating cancer" wasn't about eradicating it from his body forever. It was not about curing it. "Beating cancer" for him was a daily victory. It was about going to sleep each night and being able to say, "Today, I beat cancer." That was the victory, and he beat cancer on his terms. I could totally get behind that.

Mason had fought hard to reach that mental state and define survival on his own terms. It was his fight, his life. That's when it dawned on me that sometimes the only way to move forward is to reframe what success looks like in the present time when old definitions no longer fit.

When we refer to a dream career, we often fall into easy definitions. We are taught to be successful in terms of titles, salary ranges, and LinkedIn accomplishments, among other metrics. For many of us, a "dream career" is often associated with prestige, a big bank account, and a corner office. However, once illness happens, those definitions can begin to feel adversarial.

That certainly does not mean you cannot have a dream. I want you to dream so hard you start to sweat while reading this book. I just mean that the dream may blur and morph into something else. It may no longer be about climbing the corporate ladder or following the career plan you made years ago. It's about finding a way to contribute, create, or support yourself in a manner that aligns with your body's needs, rather than constantly fighting against them. It's about finding work that, well, *works.* (I'm sure I'll win a Pulitzer for this.)

Redefining your dream may feel like you're settling. I get it. I urge you to exercise reframing. Mold and shift the dream into a new shape that feels right. We're aiming for victories you can celebrate every single day, just like Mason did with cancer.

This isn't something that happens overnight. You don't quit your job on Friday and launch your chronic career hustle on Monday. This is a marathon, not a sprint. It takes time. It takes trial and error. It requires patience, persistence, and a willingness to continually adjust as you progress.

That's what we're going to do here. We're going to take this in stages. First, there's the spark, that tiny whisper of an idea that makes you wonder, "What if?" Then comes the blueprint, when you start putting together a plan—an actual, actionable strategy to get from where you are now to where you want to be. Next is the foundation; this is where you test the waters with side gigs, training, or part-time work before diving in. Eventually, we can turn those small steps into something sustainable. And finally, we'll acknowledge the part where you realize that nothing is set in stone. There will inevitably be bumps in the road. We'll discuss how to give yourself permission to pivot, scale back, or shift gears when necessary.

Throughout this book, please remember that this is your story. No one else gets to define what your flare-friendly future looks like. Not society. Not your family. Not some outdated vision of success that no longer fits your reality. We will find what works for you, whether it's remote work, freelancing, a creative side hustle, or something entirely different.

By the end of this book, you'll have the tools to start building that path brick by brick, day by day. It may not look like anyone else's path or what you originally envisioned.

But it will be yours.

And that's what matters.

Reshape the Traditional Career Mold

For most of our lives, we've been fed a particular version of what the ideal career looks like. It goes something like this:

- Graduate from high school, college, or trade school.
- Land a stable 9-to-5 or trade job with benefits and a clear career trajectory.
- Stay in that job (or one just like it) for 40+ years, collecting promotions, pay raises, and maybe a gaudy plaque at retirement.

- Afford to buy a home, have a family, and live the American Dream™.

Sounds rad. Sounds secure.

For someone managing a chronic illness, sounds like absolute nonsense.

That version of success is built on outdated societal standards that never accounted for disabled, neurodivergent, or chronically ill professionals. It assumes your body will be able to clock in at 8 a.m. every day, sit at a desk for eight hours or work a physical job, and maintain that consistency for decades. It assumes you'll be able to push through bad days because everyone is tired, right? Ugh.

A traditional full-time job assumes you can work consistent hours, five days a week, every week. It assumes you won't need unexpected time off for medical appointments, flare-ups, or sheer exhaustion. It assumes you can function at full capacity every day, regardless of pain, brain fog, or fatigue. And when you can't meet those expectations, it labels you as unreliable, difficult, or not a "team player."

For many of us, the standard career path is a constant battle between proving our worth and hiding our limitations. We push through bad days out of fear of being seen as weak. We overwork when we feel good because we don't know when our next bad day will hit. We juggle guilt, exhaustion, and the creeping worry that we're always one sick day away from losing everything.

So maybe it's time to stop forcing ourselves to play a game that wasn't designed for us in the first place. This is where flexible, adaptable careers come in. Careers that don't punish you for needing rest, that let you set your own schedule, and that work with your energy levels instead of demanding more than you can give. These career paths don't have to be second-rate or some disappointing compromise. They could offer more stability, freedom, and sustainability than a traditional full-time job ever could.

That definition of career success doesn't work for a lot of people anymore—even so-called "healthy" people. The economy has shifted. Work culture has changed. Bottom line, you do not have to break yourself to fit into an outdated mold.

It's time to replace the "one good job" mindset with something that works for those of us whose bodies don't do well with rigid schedules, long commutes, and corporate nonsense. Enter the new wave of careers built with jobs (plural) that are flexible, adaptable, and, in some cases, completely self-designed.

The New Career Models That Actually Work for Us

The good news is that the traditional career path is no longer the only option. The better news is that the alternatives aren't just "side gigs" or "temporary fixes." These models are more stable, more lucrative, and way more sustainable than the standard 40-hour grind. Let's chat about some hot or emerging options.

Freelancing

I'll be totally honest with you: I'm going to be biased when it comes to freelancing. This is my jam. My bread and butter. My sweet home Alabama. Leaving corporate America to start my digital marketing business, which essentially meant freelancing, was one of the best decisions I made during my career. I have taken freelance gigs ranging from copywriting to social media management, and sports writing to content management. Unless I was occasionally desperate for a paycheck, it has allowed me to choose the jobs that I wanted to take and with whom I wanted to work.

Instead of being tied to a single employer with fixed hours, freelancers can work for multiple clients, selecting projects that align with their skills, interests, and energy levels. If you have a bad week, you can take on fewer assignments. If you need a flexible schedule, you can build one that accommodates your needs. And if you want to sometimes work until midnight? You can do that, too!

While it pains me to point out the downsides, there are some drawbacks to consider. No guaranteed paycheck, which is scary as heck when you have medical bills to pay. Additionally, it takes time to establish steady work. This can require networking if you don't already have one based in your field of interest. And that's about as fun as kidney stones for most of us pajama enthusiasts.

We're going to explore the freelance world in much more detail soon, but to start, here are some early things to consider:

Opportunities:

- Control over workload and schedule – Work when your energy allows, and rest when you need it.
- Diverse income streams – Multiple clients mean you're not reliant on one employer.

- Work from anywhere – Most freelance work is remote-friendly, cutting out commutes. I've worked at campgrounds (fun!) and doctors' offices (hey, as long as I gotta sit there, I might was well earn some cash, right?).
- No office politics – You choose whom you work with and what projects to take on.
- Easier to scale up or down – Can take on more work when feeling good, scale back when health declines.

Barriers:

- Income inconsistency – Paychecks aren't guaranteed; work ebbs and flows.
- No employer benefits – No paid sick leave, retirement plans, or employer health insurance.
- Client unpredictability – Some clients ghost, delay payments, or are just plain difficult.
- Self-discipline required – No boss to hold you accountable, which can be tough when dealing with brain fog or fatigue.
- Upfront hustle – It takes time to build a steady stream of clients and a reputation.

Multipotentialite Careers

A multipotentialite is someone who refuses to be boxed into just one career identity. They've got range. They're the kind of person who's good at more than one thing and curious enough to chase after them. If this is you, then instead of choosing a single track and sticking to it forever, you build a career that fits your mix of talents, interests, and instincts. Maybe you're a writer who also dabbles in tech support for seniors and social media content creation. That freedom is intoxicating for people like me who have a love affair with reinvention.

Opportunities:

- Work variety – Keeps things interesting and prevents burnout from doing the same thing every day.
- Skills flexibility – Can pivot into different fields if one industry slows down.
- Multiple income streams – Lowers financial risk by diversifying earnings.
- More creative fulfillment – Ideal for those who don't want to be stuck in one profession.
- Adaptive to health needs – Can shift between different types of work depending on energy levels.

Barriers:

- Can feel scattered – It's harder to define a career path or explain to others what you do.
- Unpredictable workload – Juggling different projects and industries can get overwhelming.
- No single employer safety net – No employer benefits, sick days, or clear career trajectory.
- More challenging to master one field – Constantly shifting between skills can make deep specialization difficult.
- May require more self-marketing – It's essential to maintain visibility across multiple industries to sustain steady work.

Portfolio Careers

A portfolio career is similar, but it pieces together multiple part-time roles, freelance projects, or contract work to form a full-time income from a single, related set of skills. For example, this could be someone who works as a freelance graphic designer, teaches graphic design part-time at a local college, and runs an Etsy shop—all for income and career diversification. The beauty of a portfolio career is that it spreads out the risk, so if one income stream dries up, you still have others to fall back on.

Opportunities:

- Diversified income – If one job or gig slows down, others can help balance finances.
- Built-in flexibility – Can mix high-energy and low-energy work to accommodate health fluctuations.
- Less career risk – Losing one part-time job or contract doesn't mean total financial disaster.
- More autonomy – More control over time management and workload.
- Opportunity for passive income – Can mix active work with side hustles like digital products or consulting.

Barriers:

- Managing multiple commitments – It can be mentally draining to juggle different roles.
- Inconsistent hours – Part-time work may not provide a steady weekly income.

- Administrative overload – More clients or employers means more invoicing, tax considerations, and scheduling.
- Harder to secure benefits – Most part-time jobs don't offer health insurance or retirement plans.
- Can feel disjointed – If roles aren't aligned, it may not feel like a cohesive career path.

Gig Work

Often dismissed as a "temporary" way to earn money, the gig economy is one of the fastest-growing work models out there. It covers a wide range of services, including freelance writing, web design, tutoring, transcription, social media management, and remote customer service. Think jobs listed on Fiverr. The key is choosing gigs that align with your skills and health needs, because app-based gig jobs like driving for Uber may not be ideal for someone with chronic pain or vision issues. But gigs that let you work from home, set your own hours, and take breaks as needed? That's a different story.

Opportunities:

- Immediate income potential – No long job search; can start earning quickly.
- Work only when able – Accept jobs based on your health and schedule.
- Diverse opportunities – Can range from writing and virtual assisting to tutoring or rideshare driving.
- No long-term commitment – Can easily stop or switch gigs if health changes.

- Suitable for supplementing other income – Can stack with a portfolio career or freelancing.

Barriers:

- Low job security – Work availability can be unpredictable.
- No benefits – No employer-provided health insurance, paid leave, or retirement options.
- Fluctuating pay – Some months may be profitable, and others may be slow.
- Platform dependency – Gig work often relies on third-party platforms (such as Upwork, Fiverr, and Uber) that take a cut of the earnings.
- May require constant job hunting – Unless you can establish repeat clients, you're always looking for the next gig.

Do you see the common threads? Top of the list is flexibility. Flexibility is a freakin' must. Some weeks, we can work full-time hours. Other weeks, we might only manage five hours. A traditional job doesn't allow for that kind of fluctuation. These career paths let us adjust our workload based on our health, but that doesn't mean the transition is always easy. Letting go of the "stable full-time job" mentality can be I-forgot-to-refill-my-prescription terrifying. It will take time to rewire that thinking, and that's okay.

Other commonality is the ability to have autonomy and control. These careers let us choose the work we take on, the clients or employers we engage with, and the pace to which we operate. They also reduce exposure to office politics and allow for more self-directed decision-making.

Lastly, the creativity and variety offered in these types of careers allow you to thrive on diverse projects. They encourage continuous growth and reinvention, which feels downright fabulous when your health journey feels stuck and stagnant.

That's the shift we're making in this book. A health-conscious hustle that doesn't overemphasize where you work or what your job title is. You deserve a career that fits like your favorite pair of stretchy pants—comfortable, flexible, and unapologetically yours.

Imagine waking up excited to pour your energy into work that aligns with your passions and values!

To help you organize your thoughts and document your first reactions, it's time for your first Work-Life Playbook. After you've finished the book, it'll be satisfying to look back at your thoughts and feelings from these early chapters. I'm pumped for you!

Work-Life Playbook

Résumé Highlights (AKA: Add this sh*t to your highlight reel.)

- A dream job is…more of a concept and less of a practical application. When chronic illness enters the chat, your version of success deserves a rewrite.
- Traditional career paths are often not built for bodies like ours, and trying to fit into them is like squeezing into my high school jeans: uncomfortable and unnecessary.
- Flexibility is the new corner office. Freelancing, gig work, portfolio careers, and multipotentialite paths aren't fallback plans—they just may be your new, fantastic future.
- Redefining success doesn't mean you've lowered your standards. It means you've finally started honoring your needs.

- You are the only one qualified to define what a badass career looks like for you. Period.

Power Moves (AKA: Do this when you're done reading and have the energy for it.)

- Write your old definition of a dream job. Now, crumple it up and toss it in the recycling bin. We're making room for something better.
- Jot down three things your body needs to function better in a work environment (flexible hours, remote work, low sensory input, etc.). These are non-negotiables for your new dream.
- Identify what you need *more of* (rest, autonomy, remote work) and what you need *less of* (commuting, micromanaging bosses, fluorescent lighting). This becomes your career compass.
- Pick one career model from this chapter that made your soul perk up a little: freelance, gig, portfolio, or multipotentialite.

CEO Mindset Check-In (AKA: Let's get real for a second.)

- What have you already survived or adapted to that proves you're capable of this transition?
- Are you chasing a version of career success you truly want, or one you think you're supposed to want?
- What would it feel like to build a job around your life instead of fitting your life around a job?

Chapter 2

Accept the Call to Adaptation and Take Action

"Am I painting a dog or a bear?"

That thought ran through my head about a dozen times while attempting to paint a picture of Flick, an insanely handsome dog who had recently crossed the rainbow bridge into the great dog park in the sky. The painting was for a friend, so I wanted it to be perfect. I had started painting portraits after grieving the loss of my beloved beagle, so I understood the importance of these memorial pieces to pet parents.

I went big on my first attempt, despite my trepidation. Black dogs are typically more difficult to paint in watercolor. They can easily look dull and flat if you don't find a way to incorporate more color, texture, and depth. I filled nearly every inch of the 8×10 paper, even including a portion of his body, which I usually don't do. Go big or go home, right?

If "home" meant a trash can, yes, I went big, and it went home. Yikes. On to attempt number two. I focused more on the face, taking more time to sketch out shadows and changes in the fur. With any pet portrait, success is in the small details. It turned out well, but I still wanted to try again. I decided to go much smaller. It's a tip I've picked up, and it really works. It forces you to abandon nuisances and conquer the basics. Painting Flick in just a little 2.5" x 4" portrait turned out really darn cute. Going small was a success!

Sometimes, going small is your only choice. April, a former police officer turned small business owner, knows all about starting with the small stuff. I interviewed her for my original career book idea, *Wishes Are for Wussies,* to learn of her devastating tale of loss and her path to redemption.

After a violent and terrifying encounter with a suspect, April was severely injured on duty. But she got up, got the bad guy, and booked him. She went home that night feeling emotionally numb, as she had for some time as a cop. She'd been trying to plan her way out of law enforcement. Despite working 13-hour days, she found time to obtain her nursing assistant certificate and planned to return to school to become a physician's assistant.

"The universe took it upon itself to redirect me," April told me.

The day after the violent arrest, April suddenly collapsed onto the office floor. She was rushed to the emergency room, where she was told she had a traumatic brain injury. At the hospital, she didn't know where she was or who she was.

After her release, April had to go back to basics. Small steps every day with a team of therapists.

"There were years that went by that I could only shower or get dressed with post-it notes of instruction," she explained.

"The hardest part was looking normal from the outside, like at the grocery store. You're standing in line, and you can't figure out how to count money, and people are yelling at you."

As she started to get stronger, the universe nudged her again. This time in the form of a bad bra fitting. That's right, you heard me, a series of ill-fitting over-the-shoulder boulder holders. She couldn't find a fit that worked. Each bra she tried on left her more and more discouraged. And to make matters worse, the attendant was only adding to the frustrating moment. It was the bra strap that broke the camel's back.

"Now is not the time for people trying to make me feel bad!" The thought screamed into April's head and took root. Then another thought appeared: "There must be other women who feel the same way."

The small seed for her lingerie business was planted. Over a couple of years, she took manageable action steps to launch a business that allowed her to control her environment and pace, which was still key to her recovery. She conducted research, interviewed experts, attended trade shows, and more to ensure proficiency in all aspects of lingerie and undergarments.

Fast forward a few years, and her shop is thriving. And it all started with accepting the call to adapt.

Signs It's Time to Make a Career Change

For many of us health-impaired folks, there comes a point when you realize the career you once thrived in (or at least tolerated for the paycheck) is now actively trying to ruin your life. It could be the soul-crushing fatigue that turns your morning routine into a Herculean task. Maybe it's the chronic pain that makes sitting at a desk for eight hours feel like some medieval form of torture. Perhaps it's the GI system from hell that puts you in the public stall four times a day with a mini-size of Poo-Pourri. Maybe it's just the deep, gut-level understanding that your body isn't on board with this job anymore, and something has to give.

That moment? That's the call to adaptation. And let me tell you, it's an infuriating one when you have enough heavy decisions on your plate, which we often do when managing health concerns.

If you're anything like me, your first instinct might be to ignore it. To push through. To tell yourself, *I can make this work. I just need a better chair, another cup of coffee, to eat cleaner, or maybe if I sleep for 14 hours straight, tomorrow will be better.*

We all know it won't (or at least not permanently). Because a nap or a lumbar support pillow isn't the forever fix.

I fought this realization hard. I told myself I was just going through a rough patch and that things would get better if I could manage my schedule a little differently. I was already running my own business and working from home, so I thought, "Come on, how hard could this be?" However, the truth was that no amount of time management hacks could change the fact that my body had staged a full-on rebellion against my 40+ hour workweek model. I can recall days prying myself away from my bed, waddling in pain to my home office, working for an hour, and being so exhausted that I could cry. I'd shuffle to the couch and instantly fall back asleep for a couple of hours. This was *not* ideal when I had full-time contracts with numerous deadlines to manage.

So, how do you know if you're at that breaking point? How do you differentiate between "I'm having a tough week" and "This job is actively making my chronic illness worse"?

If you're nodding along to most of the below, it might be time to start planning an exit strategy:

- Your job is making your symptoms worse, not just stressing you out. Everyone has bad days, but if your job is causing regular, severe flare-ups or making it impossible to manage your condition, that's a sign your work environment is incompatible with your health.
- You're spending more energy trying to survive work than doing work. If just getting through the day leaves you so drained that you have nothing left for your personal life, your job is taking more than it's giving.
- You constantly worry about being seen as unreliable. You might find yourself lying awake at night, stressing about how many sick days you've taken. You wonder if your boss is doubting your authenticity, which puts you in constant defense mode.
- Accommodations feel like a battle. If every reasonable request for flexibility, remote work, or schedule adjustments turns into a fight, you have to ask yourself: *Is this job worth the exhaustion of constantly advocating for basic needs?*
- You daydream about alternative careers, but you never let yourself take it seriously. If you keep thinking about freelancing, remote work, or some other flexible career path but dismiss it immediately as "not realistic," it's time to ask yourself why. (And also, hello!—this book exists to tell you that it *is* realistic.)

- You're burnt out in a way that no amount of rest can fix. If a long weekend or vacation doesn't even begin to put a dent in your exhaustion, you're not just tired—you're in full-blown "this isn't sustainable" territory.

If these signs sound familiar, then congratulations (and also, I'm sorry) because you're officially at the career reevaluation phase of chronic illness. It's as stressful as waiting 8 months for a new patient appointment, I know. But ignoring it won't make it go away.

The Mental Hurdles of Accepting Change and Overcoming Self-Sabotage

Alright, you've come to the gut-wrenching realization that your current career is about as compatible with your chronic illness as a cat is with a bubble bath. You're not alone in this; many face the daunting task of reevaluating their professional lives in light of health challenges. But change is freakin' hard.

Like many of you, my diagnosis journey was like a bad thriller movie. Just when I thought I solved the mystery, I would get dismissed by another provider, hit with another normal test, and riddled with a new symptom. I think it took me so long to change my business model because I had gaslighting doctors' voices in my head, "Nothing is wrong with you. Quit seeking specialists and move on with your life." How could I justify cutting my contracts and changing how I vet potential clients based on that? With the help of therapy, I learned to trust my inner voice, not the outside voices that haunted me. Trusting your gut is more likely to serve you better than damaging (and useless) rhetoric from others.

Embarking on a career shift is a profound psychological journey, fraught with mental hurdles that can make or break your transition. Let's delve into these challenges, backed by psychological insights, and explore how to navigate them without losing your sanity—or your sense of humor.

The Comfort Zone: Your Personal Bermuda Triangle

First up is the infamous "comfort zone." It's that cozy, familiar space where everything is predictable, even if it's slowly sucking the life out of you. Venturing beyond it feels like stepping into the Bermuda Triangle—who knows what horrors await?

Psychologically, this is tied to our brain's preference for familiarity. According to the American Psychological Association, our brains are wired to favor predictable outcomes over unknown ones, even if the current situation is detrimental to our well-being. This preference can keep us stuck in unfulfilling careers, as the fear of the unknown outweighs the discomfort of the present.

Tip: Start by making small changes within your current role to build confidence. Think of it as dipping your toes into the change pool before committing to a full dive. Before I got sick and considered leaving my traditional job for a freelance life, I started very small. I took a part-time contract that I could easily do on weekends. Now, don't grumble at me; I know I wasn't completely drowning in turbulent autoimmune oceans at that time, but I did have hEDS. Was it sometimes tough to work a full-time job and a contract job in my free time? Sure. However, it allowed me to test the waters before fully committing.

The Fear Factor: When "What Ifs" Attack

Ah, fear—the ultimate party pooper. What if you fail? What if the new career is worse? What if you can't afford your marketplace insurance? What if your marketplace insurance sucks? What if you end up living in a van down by the river?

Fear of failure is a significant barrier to change. A study published in the *Journal of Business Venturing* found that fear of failure can inhibit individuals from pursuing new career opportunities, even when they are dissatisfied with their current situation. If this is how you feel, please know you are not alone.

Tip: Reframe failure as a learning opportunity. Remember, even Thomas Edison had a few dud lightbulbs before he got it right. I accepted contracts numerous times that I had zero business taking on before I realized I can't do this anymore. It took some practice before I started to stick the landing by saying "no" or "not right now" to potential work.

Analysis Paralysis: The Art of Overthinking

You've made your pros and cons list, color-coded it, and cross-referenced it with astrological charts. Yet, you're still stuck. Welcome to analysis paralysis, where overthinking leads to inaction. This occurs when individuals overanalyze or overthink a situation, causing forward motion or decision-making to become "paralyzed," meaning that no solution or course of action is decided upon. A study in the *Harvard Business Review* highlighted that excessive information gathering can lead to decision paralysis, preventing action.

I would drive my husband nuts with this. I'd tell him about a potential client who reached out, explaining that it would be a lucrative job, but I had a gut feeling it would drain me.

"There, you have your answer," he would say.

Oh, how he underestimated my brain. I'd obsessively think about it nonstop. What if I could do it? What if I couldn't? What stopped the endless loop of thoughts? Having confidence in myself. I had to trust that I was doing what was best for my health, and that decision had a very positive domino effect. I perfected the art of fielding clients so that I was always only taking on high-paying, low-stress work.

Tip: Set a decision deadline. Give yourself a reasonable timeframe to gather information, create a cost-benefit analysis (also known as a pros-and-cons list), and then make a choice and commit to it. Remember, even not making a decision is a decision.

The Identity Crisis: Who Am I Without My Job Title?

I'll bet that for years, your identity has been closely tied to your job title. I used to feel that way too. Letting go feels like erasing a part of yourself. This identity crisis can be a significant mental hurdle.

According to Erik Erikson's stages of psychosocial development, our careers often play a crucial role in our sense of identity and purpose. A career change can disrupt this sense, leading to confusion and anxiety.

I went from proudly saying I was a social media manager at an international nonprofit to a digital marketing business owner to a part-time patient advocate, part-time content manager, and writer when I can. Yes, some people may be more impressed by my first two titles compared to my hodgepodge of gigs. As Mel

Robbins would say, "Let them." Let them feel that way. I love my patchwork of roles and I know I play an important role for those with whom I work.

Tip: Engage in self-reflection to explore other facets of your identity. Are you a proud mom or dad? Auntie or uncle? Are you a caretaker extraordinaire to your pets? Do your friends think you are the bee's knees? You're more than your job title—unless your job title is "Supreme Overlord," in which case, carry on.

The Sunk Cost Fallacy: Throwing Good Time After Bad

You've invested years, maybe decades, into your current career. Walking away now feels like throwing all that time and effort down the drain. This is an example of the sunk cost fallacy in action.

The sunk cost fallacy refers to the tendency to continue an endeavor once an investment of money, effort, or time has been made. A study in the *Psychological Bulletin* found that many people are prone to this fallacy, often leading them to persist in unfulfilling careers due to past investments.

Tip: Focus on future benefits rather than past investments. Ask yourself, "What will make me happier and healthier in the long run?" Also, remember that life experiences and work skills are never truly lost. They will often provide a fantastic foundation for your next chapter.

The Imposter Syndrome: Waiting for the Fraud Police

You're considering a new career path, but a little voice in your head whispers, "Who do you think you are?" This is imposter syndrome, where you doubt your abilities and fear being exposed as a fraud.

Imposter syndrome is a psychological pattern where individuals doubt their accomplishments and have a persistent fear of being exposed as a "fraud." Research published in the *International Journal of Behavioral Science* indicates that up to 70 percent of people experience imposter syndrome at some point in their careers.

This crippled me when I was trying to decide whether to go back to school to study to become a board certified patient advocate. It took me four years to get diagnosed with Sjogren's disease and five years for a myasthenia gravis diagnosis. Who was I to help people on their diagnostic journeys? Create a course on Sjogren's? Who do you think you are? Not some world-class rheumatologist researching the disease. Sit down. I had more therapy sessions than I could count tackling imposter syndrome. Ultimately, I came to realize that my experiences could be beneficial to others, especially when combined with formal education. I may not be able to diagnose a patient or fix a broken healthcare system, but I could confidently provide empathy, support, and strategies to improve their journey.

Tip: Keep a "brag file" of your achievements and positive feedback. When doubt creeps in, refer to it as a reminder of your capabilities. For the areas you do feel aren't as strong, brainstorm ways to boost those skills to elevate your confidence.

The Social Mirror: Worrying About Others' Opinions

"What will people think?" This question has killed more dreams than failure ever could. The social mirror reflects our tendency to base our decisions on others' perceptions of us.

Social psychologist Charles Cooley introduced the concept of the "looking-glass self," where our self-concept is shaped by how we believe others perceive us. This can lead to decisions that prioritize others' opinions over our own well-being.

I have a friend with a master's degree and over a decade of business experience, but she was utterly miserable at her job. Anxiety through the roof was taking a substantial toll on her mental health. One day, I got her to name a job she thought she would like, and to my delight, she said, "florist."

"That sounds amazing!" There are so many classes out there for that. Let's find one and sign up!" I said to her.

"I can't work at a flower shop. I have a master's degree. What would people think?" she worried. And sure, her worries extended to money and benefits. But who knows? Perhaps being a part-time florist could have evolved into her own shop down the road, as she had the business skills to make it happen.

Maybe staying the course was right for her—only she can know that, but it broke my heart to think she threw away a chance at a soul-fulfilling, creative job largely because of the opinions of others.

Tip: Practice self-compassion and prioritize your needs. As the saying goes, "Those who mind don't matter, and those who matter don't mind."

The Perfection Trap: Waiting for the Stars to Align

You're ready to make a change, but you tell yourself the time must be right: the economy must be booming, your health significantly better, and pigs flying.

This perfectionism can keep you stuck indefinitely.

Perfectionism involves setting excessively high standards and being overly self-critical. According to the *American Psychological Association*, perfectionism is linked to anxiety and can hinder decision-making and progress.

Tip: Embrace the concept of "good enough." I mean, we practice "good enough" in healthcare all the time, don't we? We should be pros. Put this on repeat in your noggin: Progress is better than perfection. Waiting for the perfect moment often means waiting forever.

Moving From Being Overwhelmed to Taking Action

By now, you may be feeling a tad overwhelmed. Maybe you've accepted inevitable change gracefully, like a wise sage who welcomes transition with open arms. Or perhaps you've ugly-cried in your car, stress-eaten an entire bag of chips, and convinced yourself that you can just push through for a few more years (even though you doubt that). Either way, you've arrived at the part where it's time to stop spiraling and consider a plan of action.

Career changes, especially ones that involve freelancing, portfolio careers, or multiple income streams, are not things you just jump into on a whim (unless you enjoy the thrill of financial instability). They take planning, patience, and a strategy. And that strategy needs to be executed in a way that doesn't wreck your already overworked nervous system. So, let's break down how to get you from overwhelmed to "I've got a plan."

Step 1: What Kind of Work Life Do You Want?

Before we do anything, let's brainstorm what you're considering building. If you're going to put in the effort to create a career that works for your body, mind, and bank account, you need to understand what that may look like.

Take a minute to answer these seven questions (seriously, write them down) and take your time soul-searching:

1. Do you want complete flexibility, or do you need some structure? (Ex: completely self-employed with a variety of projects vs. ongoing remote job with one employer)

2. Do you want multiple income streams or just one main gig? (Ex: portfolio career vs. focusing on one business)

3. What kind of work do you enjoy that also works with your health? (Ex: writing, virtual assisting, design, consulting, coaching, etc.)

4. How many hours per week do you realistically have the energy to work on average? (Not what you *wish* you could do, rather what you *can* do.)

5. Do you need to work from home, or can you handle some in-person work?

6. Are you comfortable with the unpredictability of freelance work, or do you need some stability? (Ex: retainer clients, contract work, part-time job)

7. How do you prefer to get health insurance? No worries if you don't know the answer to this as we have a whole chapter on this topic later. (Ex: through a spouse, ACA marketplace, COBRA, Medicaid buy-in)

Your answers will help determine what kind of career transition makes the most sense. A portfolio career might be perfect if you like variety and multiple income streams, but if uncertainty gives you hives, you may want something with more predictable income, like contract work or a part-time remote job mixed with freelancing.

Step 2: The Money Talk—Planning Your Finances

No one loves talking about finances (I'm practically allergic to numbers), but unless you plan on surviving off vibes and hope, you need to crunch some numbers before making any big career moves.

How much money do you sincerely need? Time to grab a calculator and your bank statements. Answer the following:

1. What are your *absolute minimum* monthly expenses? (Rent/mortgage, groceries, insurance, medical costs, utilities, transportation, etc.)

2. What are your *actual* monthly expenses? (Include fun things like streaming services, takeout, hobbies, etc.)

3. What's your ideal "comfortable" monthly income goal?

4. How much do you have in savings?

5. How much should you have before transitioning to a new career? (Generally, 3-6 months of living expenses are smart for freelancers, but this depends on your risk tolerance and other financial safety nets.)

Now, let's talk about salary goals. Once you know how much you need per month, you need to figure out how much you need to earn per hour to make that happen.

Use this formula:

[Monthly income goal] ÷ [hours per month you can work] = Minimum hourly rate

But wait—taxes, business expenses, and health insurance exist whether we like it or not. Freelancers and gigsters should add 30-35 percent more to account for taxes and overhead.

Example:

- You need $3,000 per month to cover expenses.
- You can realistically work 80 hours/month (20 hours/week).
- $3,000 ÷ 80 = $37.50/hour (before taxes).
- Add 35 percent for taxes & expenses → $50.63/hour.

To cover your living expenses while accounting for taxes and business costs, your minimum hourly rate should be around $51/hour.

You may be thinking, "Who the heck is going to pay me $51.00 an hour?" When I started my business and pitching proposals, I agonized over my hourly or package rates. Yes, I had ten years of marketing experience at the time. I was not a newbie, but I didn't think anyone would legit pay me some of the industry rates I saw (we're talking $100 per hour).

My point of contact at one of my most consistent early contracts (I was pulled in multiple times when they were short-staffed) shared one of the greatest nuggets of wisdom with me. Sadly, the company was doing some restructuring, and she was laid off. With a "nothing-to-lose" mentality, she pulled me aside and told me that I was the hardest-working contractor at the company with the lowest hourly rate.

"You need to raise your hourly rate by at least $20 an hour for the work you deliver," she advised.

While it was one of the best compliments and pieces of advice I got, I didn't think there was any way people would pay that. But I did trust her and respected her as a leader. When the next potential client reached out to me, I said the new hourly wage as if it had been that price for years. *Totally normal. Nothing to see here.* I thought while sweating profusely.

"Sounds great. When can you start?"

My dysfunctional jaw hit the floor. That lesson learned before falling ill provided the foundation for later working limited hours at a higher rate. When considering the costs of traditional employees, companies must pay for medical insurance, disability insurance in some cases, offer vacation and sick leave, and spend weeks onboarding. There are a lot of costs involved for full-time employees. While the hourly rate may seem astronomical, the overall cost of a freelancer is much cheaper.

Step 3: Business Basics—What You Need to Set Up

If your new career involves freelancing, coaching, consulting, or anything where clients pay you directly, you'll need to handle business logistics. We do dive deeper into finances and business needs later on, but I want you to start thinking about it.

Decide on a Business Structure:

- LLC vs. Sole Proprietor: LLCs offer legal protection but cost money to set up; sole proprietors don't require formal registration, but you're personally liable for everything.
- Do you need a business license? Depends on your state and the type of work you do. Check local regulations.
- Does your town require a home office permit?

Do You Need Business Insurance?

- If your work involves consulting, coaching, or handling sensitive data, liability insurance may be a smart investment.
- If you sell physical products, product liability insurance is a must.

Upfront Costs to Consider:

- Website domain and hosting (if you need a personal site)
- Design software or subscriptions (Adobe, Canva Pro, Notion, etc.)
- Marketing materials (Business cards, social media ads)
- Online course platforms (If you're creating digital products or teaching)

Step 4: The Transition Plan—How to Build While You Work (and Stay Sane)

Unless you've got a magic money tree, you probably can't quit your job tomorrow and hope freelancing works out. So, how do you transition without imploding your finances? Take these six steps:

1. Start with Small Gigs: Take on one or two freelance projects while still employed. I know it isn't always possible when you're unwell, but ideally, you would dip a Raynaud's toe in the water.

2. Build Your Client or Customer Base Gradually: One solid client leads to another. Let it snowball.

3. Save Aggressively: Put all side income into a business savings account as a buffer. Cancel Amazon Video. Buy generic

brands at the grocery store. Kick that soda pop habit. These are (hopefully) temporary sacrifices for long-term joy.

4. Set a Transition Goal: This may sound like, "Once I'm making 50 percent of my salary from freelancing for three months, I'll go full-time."

5. Secure a Safety Net: Make sure you have a health insurance plan lined up before quitting.

6. Give Yourself an Exit Date: Without a clear goal, you'll stay stuck in limbo.

Right now, this might feel like a lot. But you don't have to do everything at once. You just need to start.

Work-Life Playbook

Résumé Highlights

- Career change due to chronic illness isn't just a practical decision; it's an emotional and psychological process that deserves patience, compassion, and a little therapy.
- Sometimes, "go big or go home" means going small and tossing your first draft in the trash. Progress often starts messy.
- There are real psychological reasons change feels impossible: perfectionism, imposter syndrome, fear of failure, sunk cost fallacy, social pressure—we're not imagining it. But we're also not letting it win.
- Change doesn't have to be impulsive or total chaos. You can plan, pivot, and protect your peace while moving forward.

Power Moves

- Start with a micro-move. Research one job or gig that would work better for your health. This can just be

Googling "freelance jobs that don't involve serving people." No pressure!

- Make a "can-do list" that's based on your current energy, strengths, and situation. Not what you wish you could do, but what's possible right now.
- Research online courses, certifications, or micro-skills that interest you, because even one hour of learning something new is a win. And YouTube totally counts.

CEO Mindset Check-In

- Am I confusing "giving up" with "getting real"?
- What would I tell a friend if they were feeling the way I do about my job right now?
- If I gave myself permission to start small—like really small—what could that look like this week?

Chapter 3

Know Thyself, Know Thy Limits

It was supposed to be a quick sick day for Sara. Actually, not even a day. She had taken the morning off from teaching her second-grade class. It was just enough time to swing by the doctor and hopefully get an explanation for the strange fatigue, the weight loss, and the overall feeling that something was off. She'd planned to be back in her classroom by lunch.

Instead of returning to snack packs and recess, the doctor gave her two options: call an ambulance or have someone drive her straight to the hospital.

Her blood sugar was so high that it didn't even register on the glucometer.

"I was like, no—you don't understand. I have to be back at school. My kids are expecting me. I only have a sub until 11:30am."

But this wasn't optional. "Ma'am," the doctor had said firmly. "You're not going anywhere except the hospital."

In the end, her stepmom came to drive her. Sara had been teaching that morning. She had driven herself to the appointment. "Cognitively, I felt fine," she said. "I had the physical symptoms, sure, but I had no idea what was going on."

This dedicated teacher was 24 years old, and that day, she was admitted to the hospital for Type 1 diabetes. And that's where she stayed for a week.

The timing couldn't have been worse. Although, when is it ever great, right? State testing loomed the following week. Her classroom of second graders were already nervous about their first standardized exam. Even lying in a hospital bed, a voice inside her whispered: *You don't have time for this. You can't let them down.*

So the very day after discharge—still fragile and learning how to calculate carbs and count insulin units—Sara returned to her classroom.

"Looking back, that was a horrible decision. But I just felt that pressure to perform at the exact same standards. And I wasn't going to let this disease define who I was."

Unfortunately, chronic illness has a way of throwing your best intentions into the woodchipper.

She couldn't have known just how relentless the management of Type 1 diabetes would be. "I was so ignorant about diabetes," she said. "I just thought you took a pill, and you're fine. Okay, sure, you gotta cut out some sugar…don't eat the cupcake, whatever."

Talk about relatable. It is a common phase folks with chronic illness seem to experience.

"I have to check this every two hours," she explained. "I have to prick myself every two hours. I have to go into this bathroom and do this, and I just gave myself a shot, and okay, what's my blood sugar? And I can't eat for forty-five minutes. However, this is my lunch period, and I really have to go to the bathroom, but I can't because I have these kids in this room, and I can't find someone to cover for me to go."

My head was spinning just listening to how she had to manage it all.

Over time, even her students began to recognize the sounds of her devices. "They knew the different kinds of beeps," she said. "If it's the long, stagnant beep, they'd go get help or tell another teacher." They even became educated in diabetes, which I thought was very cool.

"They always knew if I was drinking a juice box, it meant my blood sugar was low. It wasn't that I was having a snack, and they couldn't."

She continued teaching despite blood sugar crashes and dizzy spells, pushing through with quiet urgency and a deep sense of responsibility to her students.

What Sara didn't fully acknowledge until much later was that she had been pushing through dangerous lows for years. "I'd just drink the juice and keep teaching. I never gave myself time to recover. I was so determined to appear normal. To not use my diagnosis as an excuse. I became hyper-independent."

She was promoted to assistant principal, but it certainly didn't ease her stress or intense schedule. Trying to balance responsibility with the demands of her health was a constant battle. And she lived like that for years.

It wasn't until 2021, when her family relocated to another state, that she was finally forced to pause. For the first time in her career, she couldn't find a teaching job. "It was like the only place in America without a teacher shortage," she joked.

But something shifted in that unexpected gap.

She accepted a fully remote role with a university as an academic advisor, helping college students navigate coursework and education programs. It was the first time her job allowed her to take care of herself without guilt.

"If my blood sugar dropped, I could sit on the couch for ten minutes and treat it. I didn't have to find someone to watch the classroom. I didn't have to explain it to anyone. I could take care of my body, and no one batted an eye."

For the first time, she saw just how much she had neglected herself for the sake of a career. "I came to learn that I am replaceable as an employee, but I am not replaceable as a mom and a wife and a daughter."

Today, Sara works for a very respectable division of the government in a communications role. She still supports educators, but from behind a screen. A job that comes with flexibility, autonomy, and boundaries that honor her body. She still has bad days, but those days don't break her. They just remind her to rest and listen to her body.

Looking back, she has one clear message for her younger self: "Take that short-term disability leave, girl! Use the whole summer to figure this out so that you're in a better place in the fall, and you're more comfortable and more confident with your diagnosis."

Sara's story is a masterclass in what happens when you prioritize everyone else's needs over your own and attempt to bulldoze through illness with willpower alone. She didn't slow down after a life-altering diagnosis. She didn't pause after a hospital stay. She kept teaching through blood sugar crashes and lunchless days because guilt, duty, and the desire to maintain a sense of normalcy took priority. It wasn't until she finally landed a remote job with a flexible schedule that she could see just how unsustainable her old pace had been.

"I realized how much I had abused my body throughout this journey," she said. Many of us reach this ah-ha moment through exhaustion, frustration, and a whole lot of hard lessons. If you're nodding along because this sounds way too familiar, you're not alone. This next section is for every chronically ill person who's been told (even by themselves) to "just push through" and is now paying the price. Let's talk about how to stop the cycle.

Energy Budgeting 101: Understand Energy, Self-Care, and the Art of Asking for Help

Chronic illness is like having a job where your boss is an unpredictable toddler with mood swings, and the company handbook changes daily. One day, you have the energy to take on the world, and the next, you're wondering if blinking too much is exhausting your dwindling reserves. So how exactly are you supposed to maintain a career, juggle responsibilities, and still have enough left in the tank to, you know, exist?

Enter energy budgeting!

As I discussed in my first book, self-care extends beyond bubble baths and face masks. I believe it's about knowing when to say no, figuring out what's worth your energy, and being cool with that reality.

Before we get into the action steps, let's address the reality of what happens when your energy tank is on E.

It sucks to feel like your body is holding you hostage. One of the hardest things about chronic illness is the constant tradeoffs. Do you cook a real meal tonight or save that energy so you can function for work tomorrow? Do you take on that extra client, knowing it'll pad your savings, or do you listen to your body screaming that you are not okay? Energy budgeting means making choices intentionally.

My cycle used to look like: ignore, ignore, ignore, and bam!—full-body breakdown. And every time, I would berate myself for not pacing better. If this sounds familiar, congratulations—you're human. Let's ensure you are aware of the warning signs to break the cycle.

Signs You're Not Budgeting Your Energy Well

Time to get honest with yourself. Here are some signs that your current way of doing things is not working:

- You're in a boom-and-bust cycle. One day you feel great, so you overdo it, and then you're down for three days. Rinse. Repeat.
- You're always behind. If you feel like you're always playing catch-up with work, rest, or life responsibilities, then your energy budget is out of whack.
- You feel guilty all the time. Guilt for not doing enough, guilt for saying "not now" or "never." Guilt for existing. Newsflash: You don't have to justify your energy levels to anyone.
- Your symptoms are worse than usual. If your flares, brain fog, or pain levels are consistently rising, that's a neon sign screaming, "Something needs adjusting!"
- You're borrowing energy you don't have. If you're using caffeine, adrenaline, or just stubbornness to get you through the day, you're borrowing time. Sooner or later, the collector (your body) will show up.

Part of dealing with a body that requires more ongoing attention and maintenance than you're used to is your role as its "keeper." Think of your body like a car, and you are the mechanic. I love what Sara had to say about this: "It was a reminder of how important it was to learn everything about my new diagnosis, to reflect and journal my journey to see patterns, and to not solely rely on the health care system for help. I needed someone to take charge of my new diagnosis, and I learned it had to be me. It still has to be me. Every damn day."

Learn to be an Energy Accountant

Consider your energy to be like money in a bank account. The objective is to spend wisely, conserve whenever possible, and avoid overdrafts. Do these five steps:

1. Determine Your "Salary" (Daily Energy Levels)
2. Make an Energy Spending Plan
3. Say No (Without Feeling Like a Monster)
4. Factor in Recovery Time
5. Outsource What You Can

The Art of Asking for Help Without Feeling Like a Burden

Let's talk about something many of us suck at: asking for help. Society loves to glamorize the whole "independent, never-need-anyone" thing, but no one should have to do life alone.

The key is framing your requests in a way that makes it easier for people to step up.

Instead of saying: "I have no energy for anything." (Vague, overwhelming)

Try: "Hey, could you pick up a few groceries for me today? I'm having a rough time with my symptoms." (Specific, actionable.)

Instead of: "I don't think I can do this job anymore."

Try: "I need to adjust my workload. Can we discuss what a sustainable schedule looks like?"

I'm the first to admit that I get annoyed when I passively hint at needing help and no one answers the whispering call. But we really just have to cut to the chase. People want to help; they just don't always know how. Make it clear, direct, and guilt-free.

Reconceptualizing Self-Care: The "Can-Do" vs. "Can-Not" Way

As I mentioned earlier, self-care is more than just enjoying spa days or yoga retreats. It's doing what your body needs. Sometimes that means giving yourself something (rest, hydration, a break), and sometimes that means giving something up (overworking, toxic commitments, pizza). I cover this in more detail in my first book, but the short version is this: it's unproductive and potentially harmful to focus solely on what we *can't* do. As you begin to think about how you want to reshape your career, I encourage you to continue practicing reframing and what you *can* do.

Here are examples of what that could look like:

- Can-Not: Attending a high-energy networking event in person.
  - Can-Do: Instead of attending a high-energy networking event in person, scheduling one coffee chat with one industry connection.

- Can-Not: Being on multiple video meetings per day.
  - Can-Do: Creating clear boundaries and realistic expectations before signing a contract that limits the use of video meetings.
- Can-Not: Accepting consecutive client projects with no breaks between.
  - Can-Do: Scheduling mandatory rest breaks between contracts.

It's less about giving something up and more about making space for change. There is no perfect system, and on some days, things will work out better than others. It's about learning to adjust and not insisting on pushing through until you reach your breaking point.

If you are currently feeling overwhelmed, start small. Identify just one thing you can adjust today. It could be a boundary you set, asking for help, or simply giving yourself permission to rest. And if anyone tries to make you feel guilty about prioritizing your wellness? Politely remind them that burnout is not an honorary title for them to uphold on your behalf. Then, go take a nap! You deserve it!

Work-Life Playbook

Résumé Highlights

- Pushing through isn't noble if it costs you your health.
- Chronic illness doesn't erase your ambition. Your ambition just has to learn to work with your body.
- Rest is a requirement, not a reward. You don't have to earn your right to care for yourself.

- You are replaceable at a job. You are not replaceable as a friend, partner, sibling, parent, or any other role. Let that guide your choices.

Power Moves

- Track your energy like a budget. Jot down how you felt today, what helped, and what drained you. You can't adjust what you haven't noticed.
- Can you trial-run Sara's 10-minute method the next time your body crashes? Try to give yourself permission to stop for 10 minutes. Then reassess.
- Write one script for asking for help this week. Make it clear and specific, such as: "Can you help with dinner Tuesday night?" You don't need to apologize for needing care.

CEO Mindset Check-In

- What boundaries could protect your energy if you gave yourself permission to set them?
- What would a sustainable career look like for you?
- How much of your daily routine is built for your needs vs. built for everyone else's comfort?

Chapter 4

(Re)Discover Your Superpowers

I met Kevin one Saturday afternoon at our usual spot at a
Barnes & Noble café. He pulled up in his electric wheelchair
with his usual jovial demeanor and maneuvered expertly around
tables until we found one with enough space to roll up. As we
settled in, his dad brought over drinks, placing one carefully in
front of him. Kevin activated the robotic arm on his chair using
his phone, just as he had a million times before. As an extension
of himself, he lifted the cup to his mouth with practiced ease. A
colorful "Read Banned Books" sticker on the top of the robotic
arm looked like a rebel tattoo on a bicep.

Kevin has spinal muscular atrophy, a genetic neuromuscular
disorder causing progressive muscle weakness and wasting due
to the loss of nerve cells (motor neurons) in the spinal cord. Like
many people with visible disabilities, he was never given the
option to hide it. "From day one, it was advocacy," he explained.
"First, it was my mom doing it for me. Then she taught me how

to do it myself." He recalled early barriers—preschool staff who didn't want him there and kindergarten teachers who refused to accommodate him. "That was my first lesson," he said.

Despite those roadblocks, Kevin found his way into digital media through skill, experience, and willingness to try. He was writing columns and movie reviews in college, so when he stumbled across BioNews, a media company focused on rare diseases, after graduation, he knew it might be a terrific fit.

"I just reached out to one of their columnists on Twitter," he said. That simple act of putting himself out there helped him land a role that would eventually evolve into his being named associate director of community content.

Now, he works remotely, managing forums for rare diseases, running awareness campaigns, and contributing to community columns. He does this all on a schedule that prioritizes his health and energy. "I've had friends who burned out trying to do everything. I didn't want that," he said. "I've got a setup that works, and I want to protect that."

For Kevin, success meant staying true to his desire: being creative. It also meant avoiding the pressure to perform a constant grind. "Not everything works for everyone," he said. "You've got to find what works for you."

His sight wasn't set on becoming a content strategist. And he wasn't chasing some six-figure salary, floofy title, or other boxes on a traditional career list. What he did do was follow the breadcrumbs of his own interests, and that is an excellent example to follow.

What do I mean by breadcrumbs?

In Kevin's case, it was writing. Storytelling. Connecting people. These were glimpses of what his career could be.

"I didn't go into this thinking I'd be a full-time digital media guy," he told me, casually sipping his drink, then retracting his robotic arm into place. "I just plugged into my community. I started writing, and I kept trying new things."

Those new experiences, such as speaking at conferences, evolved into a career. He knew how to stay curious, connected, and follow what worked for him. His path was paved with a deep sense of knowing himself and a willingness to try. That's how he found his superpowers: by noticing what came naturally and what felt like friction.

It's easy to lose sight of what we're good at when we're constantly worried about the logistics of it all. Not to mention that fatigue, brain fog, and years of surviving under stress can strip away confidence and blur our sense of capability. But make no mistake, you have the power to create either a full-time remote job like Kevin, or a portfolio career, or something in between. You just might need a little help seeing those skills in a new light.

Let's not start with who you used to be in a job or who other people think you should be in a job, but with the skills, instincts, and sparks that are still inside you, hidden in plain sight and ready to be reclaimed.

Discover Your Superpowers

I'm not here to tell you that you're a superhero. Toxic positivity isn't my cup of tea. I am here to tell you that you've likely got some serious career superpowers—probably more than you think. They're just buried under years of job trauma, social expectations, and that voice in your head that tells you you're not qualified to do anything outside your current, crippling box. Let's start clearing some of that false narrative out of your noggin and get you reacquainted with what you can bring to the table.

One of my favorite tools for this is *superpower sorting*. And before I get credit that I don't deserve, I want to acknowledge that this concept is similar in spirit to exercises used in coaching, therapy, and career planning—such as Ikigai, energy audits, or skill mapping—so I'm not reinventing the wheel here. I'm just giving you a version that may work when you have a chronic illness and limited energy to figure out your entire life in one afternoon.

The goal is simple: figure out which of your skills are working for you, which ones are just working you over, and which ones you should leave behind, like those jeans that you haven't fit into since the pre-pandemic era. Grab a notebook or open a blank document. You're going to start sorting your skills and experiences into five categories.

My Five Skill Categories

1. I'm great at this and I enjoy it. This is the gold. These are the skills you excel at and give you a little spark of energy. Maybe you're an excellent editor who secretly loves nitpicking over commas. Perhaps you're a natural mentor and light up when you're helping someone else find their way. Whatever it is, these are your top-tier assets—the things you want to lean into when building a flexible career.

2. I'm good at this, but it drains me. Oh yes, these exist. I'm good at social media strategy, for example. I can craft campaigns, break down analytics, build calendars, and keep a dozen content trains running on time. But if I had to do five days a week, by Wednesday I'd be bald from ripping out my hair. These are the skills you keep in your arsenal because they're useful and in demand, but they come with a cost. Use them strategically. Or better yet, find a way to package them into a service that pays well enough that you don't have to do them often. For me, this is my anchor job.

3. I'm good at this, but I hate it (or my body hates it). Listen, just because you *can* do something doesn't mean you *should*. Maybe you're a wizard with spreadsheets. Maybe your coworkers used to call you the Excel whisperer. But if it makes you feel like you're dying inside, it doesn't belong in your future plan. This category is your permission slip to stop doing the things you've outgrown or never loved to begin with.

4. I want to get better at this. This is where your curiosity lives. The things that tug at you a little. Maybe you've always been fascinated by design, or maybe you've secretly wanted to try coaching, consulting, or starting your own Etsy shop, but haven't had the time, money, or energy to explore it. That's okay; this is just a brainstorm—a list of possibilities. Come on, write it down and let it breathe. These are the areas where a little learning could unlock a new, healthier direction for your career.

5. I'm not good at this and never want to be. This is your "bless and release" category. Maybe you've tried coding and it made you want to throw your laptop out a window. Perhaps you took one project management course and realized that organizing other people's chaos is not your ministry. Own it. You don't have to be good at everything, and you certainly don't need to invest time and energy into skills that make you miserable.

Once you've sorted your skills and interests into these categories, you'll start to see patterns. You may notice that most of your energy-sucking tasks are the ones you've built your entire job around. That's valuable information. Are the things you love most the ones you've always treated as hobbies? That's good to know. You can't design a flexible, sustainable career if you don't first get honest about what fuels you and what flattens you.

So take your time with this. Be brutally honest. And when you're done, you'll have a roadmap that reflects who you are, what you need, and what you're wildly capable of creating. That's where the magic starts.

Informal Reflection

Yes, we're going to dive into the more technical and formal tools to access your superpowers; but I'm also a huge fan of the more informal detective work. You don't have to be a professional planner or a self-assessment junkie to figure out what you're good at or what lights you up. Sometimes, the simplest tools are the most powerful—especially when you're working with brain fog, fatigue, or a general sense that your whole identity has been rerouted through a GPS error.

Not every "ah-ha" moment comes from a test. Some of these moments show up when you're elbow-deep in a weird hobby, or mid-rant about your old boss, or journaling on the back of a receipt. That's why I love informal reflection tools. They're sneaky. They work in the background. And you don't need to schedule a personality debrief to use them.

One of my favorite tools? The anti-resume. I want you to make a list—not of everything you've done, but everything you *never want to do again*. What jobs, tasks, or responsibilities made you want to fake a stomach bug just to get out of them? What sucked the joy out of your day? Maybe it was the soul-crushing weekly team meeting where everyone talked in circles and nothing got done. Or was it being "voluntold" to plan office birthdays? Maybe it was client calls that dragged on for ninety minutes when they should've been an email. These details matter. Every item on that list is a clue about what not to include in your next career move.

Next, try this simple journaling prompt: *When do I feel most like myself?*

Not, "When do I feel most productive?" Not, "most helpful." Not, "most impressive."

Just *me*.

Is it when you're deep in a creative project, lost in research, or helping a friend solve a problem? How about when you're writing, painting, troubleshooting, organizing chaos, or teaching someone how to do something you've already mastered? Whatever your thing is, write it down—even if it feels silly or disconnected from your current career path. That moment of alignment? That's where the juice is. That's the stuff we want more of.

If journaling isn't your thing, you can try what I call the *highlight reel method*. This is great for anyone who's ever left a job and thought, "I'll never find anything that good again." We're going to flush that thought down the toilet, just like that one prescription that gave you a horrible rash. I want you to jot down your favorite professional memories. What projects made you feel alive? What moments gave you that hit of "I nailed it"? Was it a presentation that wowed a client? A campaign that got results? A thank-you note from a colleague? These moments are like breadcrumbs leading you to the kind of work that lights you the heck up.

Another underrated but ridiculously helpful tool is the *phone-a-friend* method. Ask the people who know you best—friends, former coworkers, your therapist—what they think you're freakin' fantastic at. Ask what roles they could see you in, what skills they admire in you, or what advice they'd come to you for. Sometimes, the clearest mirror is someone else's eyes. I know that sounds cheesy, but trust me, it's easy to overlook your own strengths when they come naturally to you.

And finally, if you're more visual, try making a *mood board* for your work life. Yep, just like Pinterest, but make it a career. What does your ideal workday feel like? What kind of space are you in? What types of tasks are you doing? Who are you helping? Is it collaborative or solo? Fast-paced or slow and thoughtful? Don't worry about job titles here. You're just capturing the vibe. Later, you can reverse engineer what kind of roles or gigs might match that energy. I created a mood board for my first book and tried to look at it every day. And I'm just sayin', that was the first book I finished after decades of attempts.

These tools are just some ways to get a clearer sense of what you want your work life to look like *now*—not what you thought you wanted ten years ago or what someone else thinks you should be doing. These are gentle ways to start peeling back the layers and rediscover the parts of yourself that got buried under the weight of illness, burnout, or just surviving.

You don't need a perfect plan. You need a few clues. And when you start following them, even if they feel small or strange or wildly impractical at first, you begin to build something that fits. That's what we're doing here. Sorting, reflecting, and reclaiming the career version of you that can thrive in the body and life you have right now.

Formal Assessments

If the idea of color-coding your feelings or journaling until the answers fall from the sky makes you roll your eyes, no worries—we've got options. There are more official, structured assessments. These are the kind you might've taken at a leadership retreat, during a team-building day, or when you were in a full-on identity crisis at 2 a.m. and fell into a personality quiz rabbit hole.

These tools aren't here to box you in or tell you that your only career path is "enthusiastic email sender." They're here to give you language to describe how you think, communicate, and thrive. And when you're trying to build a custom career that works with your body, your brain, and your actual life, that language is powerful.

The Myers-Briggs Type Indicator (MBTI).

Let's start with the classic: the Myers-Briggs Type Indicator (MBTI). This one's been around forever and is (mostly) beloved in corporate HR circles, career centers, and dating apps alike. It categorizes you into a four-letter personality type, such as INFJ or ESTP, based on how you process information, make decisions, and recharge your batteries. While it's not exactly predictive science, it can be wildly helpful in understanding whether you prefer working solo or in teams, if you're energized by brainstorming or structure, and how you deal with deadlines and pressure. Pro tip: Don't let anyone reduce you to a type. Use it as a starting point, not a finish line.

Enneagram

Next up is my personal favorite: Enneagram. This one's less about *how* you work and more about *why* you work the way you do. It taps into your core motivations, fears, and behavioral patterns. Are you a Type 1 who thrives on doing things the "right" way? A Type 2 who gains energy from helping others? A Type 5 who needs quiet time to process before diving into group chaos? Knowing your Enneagram type can help you avoid roles that drain you and lean into work that feels emotionally aligned. It's like therapy with less crying and more Instagram memes. Me? I'm a proud Type 4.

CliftonStrengths

Then there's CliftonStrengths, formerly known as StrengthsFinder. This one gets very specific and very actionable. Instead of macro personality traits, it highlights what you naturally do well—things like communication, strategy, problem-solving, and empathy. If you've ever been unsure of how to explain your value to a potential client or pitch yourself for a gig, this is gold. It gives you words and concepts to frame your strengths, which is especially helpful if chronic illness has shaken your confidence or made you forget what you're good at.

DISC Profile

The DISC profile is another one worth checking out, especially if you're planning to work with teams or manage client relationships. DISC focuses on how you behave in work environments, like whether you're more dominant, influencing, steady, or conscientious. It helps identify how you handle pressure, how you like to be communicated with, and what kind of team dynamics are ideal for you. Great for people who've been in jobs where the vibe felt off, and you couldn't figure out why.

Highly Sensitive Person (HSP) Test

And finally, the Highly Sensitive Person (HSP) test. I have a feeling many spoonies and zebras score high on this test. I know I do. If fluorescent lights make you want to scream, loud environments trigger your anxiety, or multitasking sends your nervous system into fight-or-flight mode, take this test. HSPs process sensory input more deeply than the average bear. That's not a flaw, my friend. It's a trait. Knowing you're an HSP can help you seek out low-stimulation work environments, create calming work routines, and choose roles that don't leave you fried by noon.

Each of these assessments has its pros and cons. MBTI and DISC give you great insight into your behavior and communication style, but they don't always capture nuance, and they're built on older frameworks and workplace assumptions. Enneagram goes deep into your inner world, but it can feel a little woo-woo if you're more logic-driven. CliftonStrengths is concrete and empowering, but you have to pay for the full version. HSP tests are usually free (I took it on *Psychology Today*) and quick but often overlooked in traditional career planning.

None of these tools will give you a magical career blueprint. They're not career fortune tellers (wouldn't that be nice). What they can do is help you get clearer on your needs, patterns, and strengths so that when you're evaluating opportunities, you're not guessing or shape-shifting to fit someone else's mold. And if any result makes you feel like you need to become more "dominant" or "high output" to be successful, take that as a sign to question the mold, not yourself. Use what resonates. Toss the rest.

Work-Life Playbook

Résumé Highlights

- You don't have to look or act like a "typical professional" to thrive.
- You may find your path by following your curiosity, connections, and lived experience.
- Networking comes in various formats. It could be participating in a conference or reaching out to someone via social media.

Power Moves

- Plug into your disease or disability community. Ask questions, share ideas, and be open to non-traditional paths.
- Try the "breadcrumb" method: list three things you enjoy doing or things people have complimented you on. Consider these hot leads.
- Use social media to connect with someone doing work you admire by sending a kind message, commenting on their posts, or asking a simple question.
- Pick one formal assessment to do.

CEO Mindset Check-In

- What were your formal assessment results? Did anything surprise you? What is one thing that stood out to you the most?
- Write down your answers from the five superpower sorting categories. Circle words or answers that you think you should pay particular attention to as you go through this career brainstorming phase.

Chapter 5

Identity and the Evolution of You

"Math isn't for girls." That's what Dr. Rebecca "Bexi" Lobo remembers hearing as a little girl who loved numbers and learning as much as she loved experimenting in the kitchen. While her brothers were encouraged to explore science and engineering, Bexi was encouraged to cook and sew. But when she dreamed of building a career around food, her parents made it clear they hadn't moved to America for her to "just cook." They reminded her that their sacrifices were meant to lead her somewhere they considered worthy and important.

If you've ever felt boxed in by other people's expectations, whether it's parents, culture, religion, or society, you darn well know the weight of those messages. They tell you who you are supposed to be long before you figure it out for yourself. And then chronic illness enters the picture, and the pressure is near enough to snap your painful joints.

Those early messages shaped every decision Bexi made about her education and career. She pushed herself as she was determined to prove she could excel in the sciences. She earned her BS in chemistry and a prestigious PhD in nutritional biology, but these achievements came at a price. Chasing that version of success meant setting aside her dreams of working with food and hosting her own show on the Food Network.

Her drive encompassed both a love for science and food and a determination to belong in places that once felt off-limits. That tension between the version of herself her family celebrated and the version she had quietly set aside was the fault line where her identity began to shift. The life she was building no longer felt like her own, and eventually her body forced her to stop trying to conform.

Bexi was diagnosed with Sjögren's disease years after earning her PhD, and everything she thought she knew about life started to unravel. "I didn't want the nine-to-five rat race," she told me. "I didn't want to be a status symbol for my parents." Illness forced her to reevaluate her life and ask more profound questions about how she worked, why she worked, and to whom she was trying to prove herself in the first place.

Her journey shows how deeply identity influences our choices and how factors like gender, race, culture, family expectations, and internalized beliefs shape our career paths. It also shows how these same factors can become tools for growth when we learn to understand and reshape them. Once we loosen the grip they once had on us, then we can start to honor our authentic selves. Building a career that reflects who you are means examining all of those layers and creating something that honors both your health and your humanity.

The Identity Tug-of-War

By the time Bexi completed her PhD, she had done everything expected of her. She pursued a respected career, earned a title to make her family proud, and built a life that looked successful on paper. But somewhere along the way, she realized she had been building a version of herself for other people.

"I started living for myself in my thirties," she told me. "After my PhD, I realized I had been chasing achievements for my parents and even dating for my parents. I had been no idea what Rebecca wanted."

That's a turning point many people face (chronic illness or not). That's the moment when the version of yourself that once felt secure, albeit the one shaped by external expectations, no longer feels authentic to you. And illness can add fuel to that spark; it forces you to question every layer of your identity. How much of it was shaped by outside influence, and how much is shaped purely by your own interests and passions?

Bexi calls herself a free spirit and a wild card, someone who craves spontaneity and exploration, but one still encumbered by expectation and limitation. She had envisioned a life of travel, adventure, and work that wouldn't tie her down. But fatigue, unpredictable symptoms, and new limitations shifted the ground beneath her. "I confused my family's, friends', and partners' not wanting to stay home with me for them not caring for me," she said. "I just didn't understand how sick I was. It started to be very isolating."

The tension between who she had been and who she was becoming didn't resolve overnight. It required time, reflection, and the courage to question stories she had accepted about herself. One of the most powerful tools in that process was journaling. "Writing gives unspoken feelings shape," Bexi explained. At first, she wrote the things she couldn't say out loud, not even to herself. It was a work in progress to get to the point where she could convert feelings into words and put them onto paper. Before she could write her feelings, she scribbled them. She drew them. She painted them onto the page until the shapes made space for language. Only then could she write about the anger she had toward her body, the grief over the life she thought she'd have, and the frustration of medical neglect that made her feel invisible. Over time, the act of journaling became something more than emotional release; it became a way to explore and build a new understanding of herself.

I'm someone who has been journaling for decades, but Bexi gave me a huge "ah-ha" moment. Identity work isn't simply thinking about it harder. I'm the queen of overthinking, so I can definitely say that this work goes beyond repetitive conversations in your head. Instead, you figure out more complex or unconscious thoughts and feelings by being brave enough to dig deeper by asking the tough questions. Journaling becomes a kind of laboratory for that, but only if you do it with curiosity. As Bexi put it, "Journaling only helps if you approach it with openness and curiosity. If it's just, 'Dear Diary, my day was…,' you're not going to get very far."

The turning point for her came when she stopped documenting the surface details and started giving voice to the things she usually suppressed. "I threw out all the rules and allowed myself to express myself by scribbling with so much anger and force that I tore through pages," she told me. "Only then did I find the utility in journaling and a starting point for exploration." It was the perfect experiment for this scientist.

That's the deeper purpose of journaling or any exercise of expression. For some people journaling may look like drawing, painting, singing, dancing, knitting, or a variety of other media. While the narrow spotlight is on journaling here, the broader concept refers to anything that records or captures what you're feeling and carrying.

So, whatever your platform, I'm not asking for poetic reflections or mundane documentation. I'm asking you to put words, notes, paint, or music to the things you're too afraid to express. Try to express the grief you don't want to acknowledge. Ink the resentment you've been swallowing and the fears you've avoided naming. Once those feelings exist on the page, they stop floating around your noggin like a bad earworm you can't lose. More than annoying, that earworm is more like a toxic worm at the bottom of a tequila bottle.

"Denying and/or suppressing your feelings is a form of self-gaslighting, isn't it?" Bexi asks. They become something you can look at, study, learn from, and eventually release.

If journaling hasn't felt helpful to you in the past, it may be because you were recording events rather than excavating truths. Try starting with prompts like:

- What part of my body hurts? Why does it hurt? What emotion might be buried and entwined with that physical pain?
- How can I alleviate this pain?
- What am I angry about but haven't said?
- What loss am I carrying that I haven't named?
- What part of me am I still hiding because I'm afraid of how it will be received by me or others?

If diving into writing feels intimidating or inaccessible, try visual journaling as Bexi did. Give her prompts a try:

- What color expresses what I'm feeling right now?
- What shapes match my emotions, spirals, spikes, circles, scribbles?
- What does my anger look like on paper? Is it a furious, jagged scribble that tears the page, or a soft watercolor wash gently becoming one with the paper?

I encourage you to be vulnerable, because this journaling isn't meant to be posted on Facebook or confessed to your cousin (unless you want to). It is designed to facilitate vulnerable conversations with yourself, which hopefully reveals truth.

The Intersection of Identity and Illness

Identity is rarely a single book on the shelf. It's a whole bookshelf stacked with volumes that intersect in complicated ways. Gender, race, culture, illness, and profession all sandwich together and can often shape how the world sees us and what is expected of us from an early age.

Bexi recalled one ER visit where she sat waiting, ignored and unheard. She had arrived in sweats, cognitively impaired, and unwell, but the staff acted as though she was invisible. She believes racial bias played a role in her treatment that visit—that the ER staff saw her last name, Lobo, and assumed she was a poor or uneducated Latina. It wasn't until she filed an official complaint about the encounter that her care finally changed.

Having learned that how she presented herself affected the treatment she received, she experienced a starkly different response while searching for answers about dysautonomia. After being dismissed by multiple neurologists and other providers, she arrived at her cardiology appointment dressed as though she was going to a job interview. Moreover, she came armed with a bag of salts and organized blood pressure data to help explain why she suspected she had dysautonomia and needed a tilt-table test to prove it. She introduced herself as "Dr. Lobo," and conducted herself the same way she would in a professional meeting.

She immediately noticed a difference in how she was perceived and treated. Since then, she's made a habit of approaching medical appointments the same way she would a professional meeting, not because she should have to, but because the bias she faces as a woman of color with chronic illness still shapes her medical care.

During our chat, I shared that I started bringing my husband to tough appointments because I noticed I was treated differently when he was there. Providers were more open to discussing my concerns or ordering tests. In addition to gender bias, there is also race, religion, culture, education, and age biases—all of which should have zero impact on getting the answers and care you deserve. "Should" is the key word.

If you've felt this, too, you're not imagining it. Research backs it up. Women's pain is more likely to be dismissed, people of color are more likely to be undertreated, and patients with chronic illnesses are often labeled "anxious" or "dramatic" instead of being believed. When those identities overlap, the obstacles can feel, and often are, insurmountable.

We can't dismantle these systems overnight, but we can recognize what's happening and stop internalizing the blame. "I used to think I was the problem," Bexi said. "Now I know the problem is how I'm perceived."

When we start to recognize these layered biases, we stop making them part of our story. You stop shrinking in medical appointments or job interviews because someone underestimated you. You stop thinking you're too much or not enough, when in reality you're being measured by someone else's biases. And you start advocating with the confidence that your lived experience is expertise, whether or not the person across the table sees it yet.

Rebuild Your Identity Into a Career You Love

So, how do we move reflection into action? Once you've named the tough truths on the page (or with a therapist or any other method that feels right for you), the next step is to figure out how to build a life around what really matters.

Bexi shows us exactly what this "phoenix moment" can look like. Everything started to change once she stopped living for her parents' expectations and started embracing what she wanted and needed. "I wanted control over my time," she told me. "Money was not as important as the ability to rest and do things at my own pace. That was my most important goal."

The shift from living for status to designing a life around her energy and passions became the foundation for everything that followed. A significant part of that transformation involved learning to listen to what she calls her "defiant voice." From the time she was little, when she was told that "math isn't for girls," a part of her burned to prove them wrong. That same spark carried her through each pivot and became her fuel for her reinvention.

"There's a little defiant voice inside me that likes to prove I can do something when someone says I can't. Why not embrace it?"

Trust me, I love a badass moment. Embracing a rebel voice can help you overcome the inevitable challenging moments that arise from change. A rebel voice interrupts the thought pattern of "just push through." It helps shift you from passive coping to actively directing your life. These breaking-the-norm moments may look like saying no without a three-paragraph explanation and apology. It may mean delegating a task when it doesn't align with your bandwidth. And it definitely can look like making career decisions based on your values versus other people's expectations.

These moments start to stack up. They build your confidence and improve your quality of life. As Bexi puts it, "Your life is made up of these little moments. If every little moment is one you choose and brings you joy, then, overall, you have a happy life. But if you're living for the weekend and hate what you do, that's not a happy life." No amount of weekends will fix the miserable reality of white-knuckling your way through life. Yes, work is always going to influence you in some regard, but it doesn't have to steamroll you. Honor your *self* in every small moment, and watch the whole picture shift into something sustainable.

This is where your earlier journaling comes in handy. Go back to those pages and look for themes. What values rise to the surface? What frustrations repeat themselves? What longings keep showing up, even if they scare you? These are your compass points. They're the raw material you'll use to rebuild your identity and your work life into something that sustains you.

Here are a few practices to help you bridge that gap between realization and action:

- **Define your non-negotiables.** Bexi realized she needed control of her schedule and her rest. Being rested, for example, enables her to pursue her passions. What do *you* need? Name the top three things your next chapter must include.
- **Embrace your "prove-me-wrong" energy.** Use your inner spark to fuel action. If someone says you're not qualified, too sick, or too late, gosh darn it, let that motivate you to find another way.
- **Grieve, then let go and move on.** "Bear witness to and grieve your losses," Bexi says. "But don't carry them with you, because they'll weigh you down on your road to discovery." Processing your grief clears space for what comes next.
- **Start with the life you want, not the job you think you can get.** "I mapped out what I wanted and how I wanted to spend my time and energy," Bexi shared. "Do I want to sip my coffee, luxuriate in my surroundings, and work when I feel like it? What do I want my days to feel like?" Work backwards from that vision to design career possibilities.

It also is important to acknowledge that change is hard for us *and* for those around us. When Bexi pivoted away from the career path her parents had envisioned for her and instead started her own skincare business, Bexi's Bespoke Revitalisation, it took time for them to understand. She took her training as a bench scientist and her lifelong love of food and chemistry and poured them into creating skincare formulas to heal her own skin. That expanded into creating skincare products to help people just like her. (See for yourself online—just Google Bexi's Bespoke Revitalisation and you'll find it!) She also sustains her passion for research and editing by working with Sjogren's Advocate, a comprehensive, robust online resource for Sjogren's patients.

Her mom may have struggled to accept her choices at first, but acceptance came when she saw her daughter was thriving and happy. That shift happened because Bexi stayed the course and built a life that reflected her truth. People may not understand your path right away, but often, they catch up.

Perhaps the most important reminder is that identity isn't static. It evolves with you. The story you wrote at age twenty-five might not be a good fit anymore at forty-five. Good. That means you're learning and changing. As Bexi told me, "I'm living my best life now." And it happened because she allowed herself to burn down the version of her life that wasn't authentic or sustainable, and she built something truer from the ashes.

Work-Life Playbook

Résumé Highlights

- Early messages, expectations, and cultural pressures can heavily shape identity and career choices.
- Chronic illness forces deeper reflection on motivations, values, and the life you are building.
- Journaling or expressive practices can help uncover suppressed emotions and internal truths.

- Intersectional identities (gender, race, culture, illness, profession) may influence how others perceive and treat you.
- Recognizing biases helps you stop internalizing blame and advocate more confidently.
- Identity evolves over time, and redefining your story is a normal and necessary part of growth.

Power Moves

- Give journaling or an expressive practice a try! Look for themes in your reflections.
- Define your non-negotiables for the next chapter of your life.
- Embrace your "prove-me-wrong" energy to fuel action.
- Grieve what you've lost, then release it to create space for what comes next.
- Start with the life you want and work backward to design career possibilities that fit.

CEO Mindset Check-In

- Where am I still living by someone else's expectations instead of my own?
- What parts of my identity feel outdated or no longer aligned with who I am now?
- What emotions or truths have I avoided expressing? What might they reveal?
- How have biases shaped the way I see myself?
- What small moments can I choose differently to create a life that feels more sustainable?

Chapter 6

Explore Career Possibilities

Before the shit really hit the fan with my chronic illness (intentional foreshadowing here), I had a pretty cushy job. Technically, it was an office job, but it wasn't the sit-at-your-desk-and-stare-at-Excel-all-day kind. Three times a week, I had to travel to two different teaching hospitals to meet with patients suffering with various types of muscular dystrophy, which meant lugging a heavy rolling briefcase full of materials, navigating crowded hospital hallways, and doing a whole lot of sitting in very questionable chairs. It wasn't supposed to be arduous labor, but my lower back didn't get the memo.

I complained about my back pain so much that I'm sure my coworkers wanted to shove me inside the rolling briefcase and wheel me out the door. My boss was concerned and wanted to help, so she suggested I see her chiropractor. I trusted her with my whole soul, so I took her advice and booked an appointment.

I was so ready to get the situation under control. I walked in for my new patient appointment, full of hope and anticipation that a few magical spine adjustments would solve everything. I explained my symptoms and pointed to where it hurt, and the chiropractor insisted on an X-ray. Sure, fine, whatever it takes. I walked to another room, took a few glamour shots, and waited for the results.

Eventually, I was called back into his office. It was the usual medical setup—oversized wood desk, black leather chair, framed degrees to make you feel confident that this person has, in fact, been to medical school. Across from his desk, mounted on the wall, was a lightbox where he clipped in my X-ray and flicked it on. He stared at it. Then he stared at me. Then he went back to the X-ray.

The silence stretched so long that I started to sweat. Oh my gabapentin, is something really wrong? Was I about to be diagnosed with a mysterious spinal condition? A degenerative disorder? A slipped disc? I was so sure I just needed an adjustment, but this guy looked like he was about to deliver the most shocking news of my life.

He opened his mouth, closed it, opened it again, and then finally settled on: "There's no other way to say this, but you're full of shit."

I choked on a half-gasp. "I'm sorry, what?"

He pointed to my X-ray, where every single inch of my small and large intestine was lit up white. Apparently, I was utterly, totally, alarmingly backed up.

Now, there were two reasons why I was floored by this.

One, I couldn't believe my entire back pain saga was being caused by literal constipation. I had spent months thinking I needed spinal realignment when all I really needed was, well, a different kind of movement.

Two, I had always assumed constipation meant tiny, hard rabbit poops. But that wasn't my experience at all. The only bowel movements I ever had to that point in my life were loose. If you had asked me the day before if I was constipated, I would have laughed in your face. *Obviously not!* And yet, there was hard medical evidence that my intestines were completely clogged. I had been so confident in what I thought I knew, and I had been so completely wrong. There was no mysterious, scary condition—just your run-of-the-mill constipation.

And that, my friends, is why I'm telling you this truly weird, humiliating story. Because when you go into something with preconceived notions, you might find out you're full of shit.

This chapter explores career possibilities. And if your first instinct is to say, *Oh, I can't do that. That's not for me. I don't have the skills or the talent for something like that.* I want you to pause. Because you don't know that yet. We haven't looked at your X-ray.

You may have had a previous job that has convinced you that you're only good at one thing. Maybe your illness has made you feel like your career options are shrinking by the second. But I'm here to tell you there's a lot more on the table than you think.

So, keep an open mind. There's a lot to digest. And if we find out that your assumptions are holding you back? Well, we'll get things moving.

Anchor Jobs: The Gig That Grounds You

Sometimes, people say I'm a glass-half-empty kind of girl. I disagree—I like to think of myself as a realist who just happens to sip from a very tiny, very cracked glass. That said, the various gigs and freelance jobs that make up my portfolio career have not been all sunshine and giggles.

There's one job in particular that I like to call my "anchor job." It's called an anchor because it keeps me tethered and stable. It pays most of the bills. It provides me with the most predictable security while still providing the flexibility I need. And…it also happens to be the job I like the least.

It's social media management.

Now, don't get me wrong—there are parts of it I don't hate. I get to write, which is a passion of mine. It's a skill that I've sharpened over the years, and there's always a demand for it, which makes it one of the more "in-demand" gigs in my arsenal. I also work with awesome clients. But let me tell you, being buried in the endless scroll of algorithms, trending audios, and nonstop trolls? That is the fastest route to soul-sucking burnout for me. And yet, it's the job that helps me afford groceries and medical bills. So, I stay tied to this anchor job.

When building a portfolio career or dipping your toes into the freelance world, I recommend identifying your own anchor job. This role provides you with some financial stability while you explore other, more fulfilling opportunities. It's the one job you can count on, even if it's not the one that makes you leap out of bed in the morning.

The benefits are underrated. It creates a layer of stability. It diversifies your income. It gives you permission to pursue your creative work without the pressure of paying all the bills immediately. It also provides a sense of direction when one of your other paths hits a dead end or needs a break. When one contract dries up or a client ghosts, you still have something holding you steady.

Would I love to make a living as a full-time writer with the same salary I make as a social media manager? Of course. If someone wants to fund that dream, please let me know. But right now? I'm not confident that writing alone would provide the consistent income and health-sustaining flexibility my family and I need. Therefore, I compromise.

If you're thinking about what your own anchor job could be, start by making a list of what you're willing and not willing to accept. Get brutally honest. Maybe you've been a teacher for years, but standing in front of a classroom every day is now a one-way ticket to a health crash. Could you handle being a substitute teacher instead? Could you offer tutoring sessions from home with flexible hours? Or maybe you're just burnt out on education altogether, but your skill set makes it a natural fit for now.

Maybe you're still scratching your head trying to figure out what your own anchor job could be. It's okay, you're not alone. Anchor jobs are as individual as your body's list of mystery symptoms. So here are a few fictitious examples to help you think it through:

1. The Teacher Who Couldn't Teach on Her Feet Anymore
Chronic joint pain made standing in front of a whiteboard all day a no-go. But instead of walking away from education altogether, Julie pivoted to virtual ESL tutoring as an anchor job. She teaches conversational English to students in other countries from the comfort of her bed-desk hybrid. Same skills, new setup. Bonus: no hall duty or grading late-night science projects.

2. The Nurse With a Body That Couldn't Do 12-Hour Shifts
After her autoimmune condition made hospital work impossible, Rosario picked up a steady part-time job as a telehealth case

manager. Now, she reviews patient charts from home and makes care calls in fuzzy socks. It's not the adrenaline-fueled ER life she used to live, but it gives her the structure, income, and sense of purpose she still craves.

3. The Marketing Pro Who Didn't Want to Hustle Full-Time Anymore

Nisha left the agency life behind, said goodbye to 5 p.m. panic meetings and 8 a.m. passive-aggressive Slack messages, and picked up two contract roles as a copywriter. It's not as thrilling, but it's steady. She saves the thrill for her side gig, designing hilarious merchandise for chronic illnesses on Etsy.

4. The Admin Assistant Turned Virtual Assistant

After chronic migraines made commuting a nightmare, Paul transitioned to virtual assistance. He now supports two small business owners with email management, scheduling, and calendar chaos—all from home, with a cold compress nearby and a light sensitivity filter on his screen.

5. The Hair Stylist Who Needed to Sit More Than Stand

Arthritis made standing at a salon station all day impossible, so Sasha launched a product-based anchor gig. Now, she runs an online shop selling hair care kits and tutorials specifically designed for curly-haired clients. It doesn't make her jump for joy, but it keeps the lights on while she works on launching her dream: a podcast for women navigating chronic illness and beauty.

6. The Nonprofit Staffer Who Couldn't Handle Office Life

Nonstop fundraising in-person events and back-to-back Zoom meetings weren't vibing with her energy levels anymore. Yvonne negotiated a part-time role writing grant proposals and annual reports for nonprofits she believes in. It's flexible and uses her skills, and she gets to work in pajama pants while blasting lo-fi beats.

7. The Retail Worker With a Flaring GI Tract

Sprinting to a public bathroom with a long line at the cash register just wasn't working out. Tyler leveraged their strong customer service skills to provide online product support for a wellness brand. When the bathroom calls, they can pause their work without losing their mind (or job).

An anchor job doesn't have to be glamorous or perfectly aligned with your purpose. Its goal is to hold you steady while you have things cooking on other burners. And if it happens to be a little soul-sucking? Well, that's what your passion projects and creative gigs are for. Balance, my friend. It's all about the balance.

Explore Other Types of Work

Do you have a list of career or job ideas you'd like to explore? If not, check out Chapter 14 for inspiration. Look over your list. Is something starting to stir? A tiny flicker of possibility? Maybe you jotted down "graphic designer" on your curious-but-not-committed list. Did you circle "voiceover artist" three times and underline it? Whatever it is, you've got a maybe-career swimming around your brain. Now what?

So glad you asked. It's time to play detective. No Inspector Gadget trench coat is required. But we need to conduct an investigation to determine if this career is a fit for your skills, your interests, and, most importantly, your unpredictable and often dramatic body.

Here's how to research a potential job path without getting overwhelmed, discouraged, or accidentally signing up for a $3,000 certification program that you didn't really need. Before you deep dive into every niche subreddit and obscure blog post, start with the essentials.

Three Key Questions

1. What does the job actually involve?
Find a few sample job descriptions online. Sites like Indeed, LinkedIn, Fiverr, or even We Work Remotely are full of real-world postings that will show you what employers or clients expect. Look for patterns in responsibilities—what shows up over and over again? That's your core workload.

2. What kind of training, if any, is typically required?
You don't need to go back to college for every pivot. A lot of remote-friendly jobs require zero formal education—just skill and proof you can deliver. But it's good to know if you'll need a specific certification or just a solid portfolio.

3. What do people earn in this job?
Use salary comparison sites like Glassdoor (self-reported salaries), Payscale, Bureau of Labor Statistics, or Freelance Rate Calculators (yep, they exist) to get a ballpark of what people make in this role. Keep in mind that income can vary wildly depending on the industry, location (even for remote jobs), and whether you are employed or freelance.

The Chronic Illness Checklist: What to Consider

Now that you know what the job entails for the average human, it's time to put it through the chronic illness filter. Not every job will pass this test, and that's okay. We're here to find work that works with your body, not against it. Get answers to these five questions:

1. What are the physical demands of this job?

Does it require sitting for long periods? Standing? Heavy lifting? Constant typing? Are there accessible ways to modify these tasks if needed?

2. What is the expected schedule and pace?

Is the work deadline-based or real-time? Does it allow for flexible hours, or will you need to be glued to your screen at specific times? Can you work in short bursts or only when your energy levels allow?

3. What's the noise, stress, and stimulation level?

If you have migraines, sensory sensitivities, or energy crashes, this matters. Is the work environment quiet or chaotic? Does it require multitasking or intense client interactions?

4. Can the work be done remotely?

Remote isn't just a pandemic perk for us—it's often a dealbreaker. Look for roles where 100 percent remote is an option, not just a "maybe sometimes" thing.

5. Is there room to scale up or down?

Some jobs allow you to take on more when you're feeling good and scale back during a flare. Others don't. Consider whether this job allows you to flex your energy or whether it demands consistency you can't always provide.

Use the Right Tools to Stalk Your Dream Job

Glassdoor & Indeed: Read job descriptions, salary insights, and even anonymous reviews from people doing the work.

YouTube: Search "day in the life of a [insert job here]" for an unfiltered peek into the actual workday. Spoiler: some of these are deeply cringe but weirdly helpful.

Reddit: Subreddits like r/freelance, r/digitalnomad, r/AskHR, or even condition-specific communities (such as r/ChronicIllness) often have threads featuring the jobs people are doing successfully.

Freelance Platforms: Browse FlexJobs, We Work Remotely, or Remote OK to see what kinds of opportunities are out there, and how people price their services.

Skill-building platforms: Check Skillshare, Coursera, and Udemy for courses in your area of interest. Some platforms even have job outcome data or forums where people talk about their transition stories.

Ask Someone Who's Doing the Job

This part might feel awkward, but it's one of the most valuable things you can do: reach out to someone doing the work you're curious about. You don't have to hit them with a 37-question survey. Simply send a kind and concise message, asking if they'd be open to a brief chat or email exchange about their experience.

Sample message:

"Hi [Name], I came across your profile while researching [job], and I'm curious about your path. I'm navigating a career change for health reasons and exploring options that offer flexibility. If you're open to sharing a little about your experience, I'd be really grateful."

You'll be surprised how many people are willing to help, especially if they've been in a similar boat.

Final Test: Visualize the Job in Real Life

Before you get attached to a shiny job title, run it through a reality check. Not the one in your head where everything works out perfectly, but the one where you're having a rough week, your joints feel like rusty bolts, and your brain's running on dial-up.

Picture yourself doing this job on your worst day. Can you still function? Could you scale back the workload? Could you outsource a portion of it or reschedule tasks without blowing up your income or your stress levels?

If the answer is "yes," or even, "I think I could make that work with a few tweaks," that's a good sign.

And if the answer is no? That's not a failure. That's information. You're narrowing the field. Don't be afraid to cross jobs off the list. There's freedom in knowing what *doesn't* fit. And there's power in following the trail of "maybe" jobs until one clicks.

Work-Life Playbook

Résumé Highlights

- Your current job or industry doesn't define your future. Even if your old gig made you believe you're only good at one thing, there's a buffet of jobs out there that play to your strengths and work with your body.
- Anchor jobs are underrated heroes. They might not be sexy, but they provide stability while you pursue work that lights you up or pays more long-term.

- Assumptions will hold you back faster than brain fog. You don't have to know everything to get started—you just have to be willing to get curious.
- Popular freelance, remote, and gig jobs exist across nearly every industry. From graphic design and writing to virtual assisting and SEO, there are career options for every energy level and attention span.
- You don't have to pick just one. Portfolio careers and mixed-income gigs are increasingly common and can be a strategic way to protect your income while working around flare-ups or energy slumps.

Power Moves

- Make a "Career Curiosity" list. Think through the type of work, tasks, schedules, and environments that are dealmakers or dealbreakers for your health.
- Identify your anchor job. What's a skill you can lean on that reliably brings in income, even if it doesn't bring you boundless joy? That's your financial foundation.
- Pick three flexible jobs from your list in this chapter that match your interests and strengths. Research the skills you'd need to break into each one.
- Start learning one skill that could open up a new career door. Think SEO, Canva, résumé writing, or basic coding. Free tutorials on YouTube are your friend.

CEO Mindset Check-In

- What assumptions are you making about what you can't do? Are they accurate or just based on old experiences or other people's opinions?

- If you had to describe your dream job without using a title, what would you say? What would you be doing each day? How would you feel?
- Are you turning down opportunities because you're scared of being bad at something new? What would happen if you let yourself be a beginner?
- If your body could vote on your next job, what would it veto, and what would it enthusiastically approve?

Chapter 7

How to Make Remote Work... Work

"Moo!" yelled Jonah, as I'll call him here. A maniacal grin stretched across his face as his wheelchair buzzed past me at a truly ridiculous speed. The guys at the wheelchair company had apparently decided to indulge him with settings that were almost certainly illegal for a teenager with a wheelchair. But that was Jonah—always pushing limits.

We had an understanding. I was vegan. He was allowed to tease me mercilessly by yelling "moo," and in return, I was allowed to reciprocate with pranks, like leaving baby carrots in his bed at summer MDA camp.

When I worked as the health care service coordinator for the Muscular Dystrophy Association (MDA), I got to know many of the kids and families well, especially those who attended the annual summer camp.

Even after I resigned from my position with MDA, I stayed in touch with many of the incredible families I had met, like

Jonah and his family. I attended Jonah's high school graduation. We still jabbed at each other occasionally, bonded by our mutual respect for sarcasm and playful teasing.

But when my beloved beagle of nearly sixteen years passed away, I experienced a grief that knocked the air out of me. I wasn't doing well, and Jonah noticed. He sent me a private Facebook message saying that he believed pets find their way back to us and that he *knew* this to be true. He said he had proof, and believed he meant this literally.

At the time, this fantasy was just too much. The idea of reincarnation or whatever he was hinting at felt too painful for me to process. I didn't want to imagine my beagle coming back to a world that could be so cruel to animals. I was actively involved in animal rescue work and saw cruelty far too often.

So I didn't respond to his sincere but upsetting message.

It's a choice I'll always regret.

A few years later, I got the heartbreaking news that Jonah had passed away due to complications from Duchenne Muscular Dystrophy. I attended his funeral with the former MDA director. We hugged his family and reconnected with some former camp "kids." I couldn't stop thinking about how I'd never hear him tease me again. How funny and sharp he was. And how lucky I was to have known him.

Five days later, the rescue organization I volunteer with called me. They asked if I could help with a Saturday transport from a kill shelter. It was an unusual request. Most transports are done during the week when the shelters are quieter— weekends are too chaotic for transfers.

Since my husband was off that day, I asked if he wanted to come along for his first-ever transport. He agreed. We packed the crates in the truck and made the hour-long drive to pick up two puppies. Yes—*puppies*. North Carolina ranks third in the country for euthanasia rates in shelters. It's devastating. Even puppies aren't safe. The rescues are doing everything they can, but the laws desperately need to change. Adopt, don't shop, and fix your pets!

I'll step off my soapbox.

We walked into the shelter lobby and waited as two staff members brought out the dogs. One employee handed my husband a very enthusiastic little pitbull puppy. The other gave me a fluffy golden pup that looked like he had stepped out of a Jim Henson movie. What a Muppet! He was adorable. I was sure his foster parent would be thrilled.

My husband gently loaded the pit puppy into a crate in the truck, and I kept the golden fluffball on my lap. I texted his foster: "You're going to love him. He's ridiculously cute." She asked what his name was.

I started to type, "Shelters usually don't name puppies" because they rarely do. There are just too many, and most are listed by number. Puppy 147562 or something like that. But something made me pause. I flipped through his paperwork to see if, by chance, someone had given him a name.

Sure enough, there it was—top left corner of the form, clear as day: Jonah.

"Dogs find their way back," Jonah had said. "I have proof."

I started sobbing.

I looked at my husband and said, "His name is Jonah. And he's ours." No discussion. No debate. Case closed.

I called the rescue owner and told her this was a sign, a God thing, and she had to trust me. She didn't hesitate. I texted the foster to explain, and she cried, too.

And that's how Jonah came home with us.

He turned out to be an absolute *menace*. I'm laughing as I write this. He was like a puppy on too much espresso. I know puppies are wild, but he was *wild wild*. He screamed if you tried to pick him up. He didn't sleep. Like, ever. Where were the long, cozy puppy naps people talk about? I'm convinced this was Angel Jonah's last prank on me.

Don't get me wrong. I adored my hyper little peanut. I knew he was meant to be mine. But juggling remote work, chronic illness, and a completely unhinged puppy? It was crazy town.

One desperate night, in a haze of sleep deprivation and frustration, I stumbled across an article about puppy schedules. "There are schedules for puppies?" I thought. I hadn't had a puppy in sixteen years. I was definitely rusty.

I dove into research and created a schedule based on age-appropriate puppy routines: feeding times, crate naps, training time, and bonding time. I mapped it all out hour by hour, slapped it on the fridge, and things started to change within a couple days.

The chaos calmed. I could breathe again. I could work again. And for the first time since baby Jonah barreled into our lives, I felt like I had a grip on things.

Turns out, even the most chaotic stories can shift when you find the proper structure.

Tools for Success in a Remote Work World

One of the most common mistakes made by people starting to work for themselves is a lack of a schedule. It's so easy to ping from laptop to laundry to dog walks to replying to emails to picking up the kids to crashing on the couch. Things can go straight bananas pretty dang quick. Like finding a schedule for Jonah, you have to find your rhythm and balance between work, rest, and life.

You don't have to go bonkers here. I'm not suggesting a hyper-structured, color-coded Google calendar where every fifteen minutes is accounted for, and failure to follow it results in shame and existential dread. We're not doing that. We'll build a template of sorts that you can tinker with until you find your Goldilocks just-right moment. Let's talk about how to pull that off.

Create a skeleton schedule, not a full-body cast.
I like to start with a loose structure. Think of it like scaffolding. You don't have to have every hour mapped out, but you need a general rhythm to your day. Try picking two or three anchor points: a set start time, a midday break, and a hard stop time. These give your day shape without becoming a straitjacket. For example, I usually start my day around 9:00–10:00 am because mornings are not my favorite time. I require a long warming-up period to shake off the stiffness and fatigue. I break for lunch around 1:00 pm, and I'm usually couch-surfing by 3:00 pm. After resting my eyes for 30 minutes, I usually work for another hour in a horizontal position. Sometimes I stick to it, sometimes I don't, but it keeps me from spiraling into chaos.

Honor your energy patterns.
If you know your best hours are 11:00 am to 2:00 pm, don't waste them answering emails or getting sucked into a TikTok rabbit hole. That's prime-time energy, baby. Use it for high-focus work, like strategy, meetings, or anything that requires

brain cells to fire in the right direction. Save admin stuff for your lower-energy hours. Work smarter so you can nap harder. (Coming to a t-shirt near you soon!)

Make rest non-negotiable.
This one feels counterintuitive when you're working from home and trying to "prove" you can be productive, but breaks are part of the job now. If you push through your workday without breaks, you'll end up in a flare or a full-on crash and lose days instead of minutes. Rest can mean many things: a quick lie-down in a dark room, a twenty-minute walk, guided meditation, stretching, or even watching trash TV for a brain break. But make them official. Put them on the schedule. Protect them like your rent depends on it.

Create a workspace you want to be in.
No, you don't need a Pinterest-perfect home office with an ergonomic everything and a ZZ plant named Gerald. (Okay, I do love that last idea.) You do need a setup that's functional and comfortable. If you're working from your bed, make it cozy but upright and supportive. Try pillows under your knees to take the strain off your back, for example.

If you're using a desk, ensure your screen is at eye level to avoid developing tech neck. I rotate between a standing desk (the kind that goes up and down with a press of a lever), a comfy chair with back support, and my couch, depending on how my body feels.

Bonus tip: Keep your go-to essentials within arm's reach— water, pain medication, heating pad, and noise-canceling headphones. If you're constantly getting up and down to chase things down, you're burning spoons on nonsense.

Use a task tracker that matches your brain.
Some people swear by digital tools like Asana, Notion, or Trello.
I'm old school and update my top priorities, notes from client calls,
and a running to-do list on a massive whiteboard and notebook.
Other folks prefer sticky notes, Google Drive, or even a pile of
index cards. The tool doesn't matter. What matters is that it works
for *your* brain. If brain fog is a problem, keep it ridiculously simple.
Color code if it helps. Use the same keywords. Make it fun and
functional. Don't try to force a productivity system just because
someone on Instagram swears by it.

Also, don't play in this space for too long. It's a common
trap. You spend hours setting up your task tracker, color-
coding your binders, building the perfect system, tweaking
your workflows—and at the end of the day, you haven't actually
done anything. You're knee-deep in planning mode, convincing
yourself that you're being productive when really…you're
stalling, friend. You're dressing up avoidance as organization. A
perfectly curated to-do list means nothing if you're not tackling
the actual to-dos. Planning should support the work, not
replace it. So get in, set it up, and then get to work. You can
always come back later and make it prettier if you must.

Batch your work to protect your brain.
Switching between different types of tasks can be exhausting,
especially when brain fog rolls in. Try batching similar tasks
together. Mondays for admin and scheduling. Tuesdays for
deep creative work. Wednesdays for meetings. Whatever works.
The point is to reduce the amount of energy wasted on context
switching. Your brain will thank you.

Here's a high-level look at how I batch work by the week:
week one of every month is dedicated to monthly reports,

week two is for content kick-off meetings and topic calendars, week three is for writing content, and week four is for review, proofreading, and administrative tasks like invoicing.

Set boundaries with the people who think "you work from home" means "you're available 24/7."
If I had a dollar for every time someone asked me to meet them for lunch, take a call, or chat in the middle of my work hours because "you're just at home," I'd have enough money to buy a tiny house in the woods and work in peace. Just because you're working from home doesn't mean you're not working. Your time is still valuable. You might have to remind family or friends of that more than once. It's okay to say, "I'm working from 10 to 3 today, but I can talk after that." Repeat after me: Boundaries are not rude.

Have a work-start and work-stop ritual.
When you don't leave your house to go to work, it's easy to feel like the workday never ends. This is why having a ritual to start and stop your day can help signal to your brain that it's time to shift gears. Perhaps your morning ritual involves lighting a scentless candle, filling your water bottle, and reviewing your task list. Maybe your end-of-day ritual is turning off your computer, putting on comfy clothes, and walking your dog. Doesn't have to be elaborate. Just something that marks the transition and helps your brain shut down.

Give yourself grace. Lots of it.
Some days will go sideways. Your body will revolt. A nap will replace your strategy call. You'll forget to send an invoice. You'll

miss a deadline. When those days happen—and they will—it's okay. This is not a traditional job. You are building something flexible on purpose. The whole point is to work in a way that supports your health, not despite it. Forgive yourself and move forward.

Working remotely with a chronic illness is a whole different ball game. You need to find your rhythm, create boundaries, and build a life that can hold both your ambition and your illness. A good schedule for zebras and spoonies is about creating a routine that makes you feel grounded while being Pilates-level flexible.

Tech Tools for a Health-Conscious Home Office

This is not my strong suit. Not by a long shot. When I started my home office, I tried the "wing it until it works" approach, and I definitely regret the energy and money I wasted. It is worth doing your research and giving thought to the technical side of your business. Here are some things I wish I had thought about more. And, for the love of your wallet, do your research by reading a plethora of reviews, because I'm sure my ideas will be outdated before my chin hair grows back!

Choose the right computer. Your computer is the heart of your home office. For those who prefer Apple, the MacBook Pro with the M1 chip offers a balance of power and efficiency, making it suitable for tasks ranging from video editing to managing multiple applications. If you're inclined towards a PC, Lenovo's ThinkPad series (I7 or better) is renowned for its durability and performance, making it a solid choice for small business operations. I personally love my HP Spectre.

Enhance your display. A quality monitor can reduce eye strain and improve posture. The Dell S2722QC 27-inch 4K monitor is praised for its clarity and ergonomic design. Pairing your monitor with an adjustable arm, like the Ergotron LX, allows you to position your screen at the optimal height and distance, promoting better neck and back alignment.

Optimize connectivity. Modern laptops often come with limited ports. A USB-C hub, such as the UGREEN Revodok, expands your connectivity options, allowing you to connect additional devices, including external drives or SD cards. For a more comprehensive solution, docking stations like the Dell WD19 can connect multiple peripherals and monitors, streamlining your workspace.

Prioritize ergonomics. Comfort is key. Ergonomic accessories, such as the Logitech Lift vertical mouse and Keychron Q8 keyboard, are designed to reduce strain on your wrists and hands. Investing in a standing desk can also promote movement and reduce the risks associated with prolonged sitting. I love mine because with the push of a lever, it can be transformed into either a sitting desk or a standing desk. This flexibility keeps me from being in one position for too long.

Ensure reliable internet. A stable internet connection is essential. If your Wi-Fi is inconsistent, consider using a mesh network system to eliminate dead zones, or a powerline adapter to extend your connection through your home's electrical wiring. If you have provider options, consider calling or browsing online to compare features and prices.

Manage your finances with ease. For small business owners, accounting software like QuickBooks can simplify financial management. For tracking your time, invoices and contracts, you may want to check out Bonsai, HoneyBook, Zoho Invoice, or Avaza. It's advisable to consult with a financial advisor to choose the software that best fits your business needs.

And for my fellow screen-sensitive warriors…

Get blue-light blocking glasses. If you're spending hours at a time on your laptop, using a pair of glasses that filter out blue light can make a significant difference. Look for ones with clear lenses for daytime or amber-tinted lenses if you're a night owl. I've heard good things about Felix Gray and Zenni Optical, but honestly, even a $15 pair from Amazon is better than nothing. (Bonus: they hide under-eye bags from all those sleep-deprived nights.)

Enable night mode or blue light filters on all devices. Most phones and computers now have built-in blue light filters. On Windows, it's called Night Light. On Macs, it's Night Shift. Android and iPhone both have blue light and "eye comfort" modes. Whatever you have, turn it on and leave it on. Your eyes will thank you.

If you want more control, check out free apps like f.lux, which adjusts your screen's color temperature based on the time of day and your sensitivity to light. Want even more options? IrisTech offers advanced settings and specialized modes for enhanced medical sensitivity.

Go matte or go mad. If you're working near windows or under fluorescent lighting, glare can mess with your eyes big time. A simple matte screen protector or anti-glare filter can reduce reflections, minimize squinting, and make your screen feel a little less like staring into the sun. Some also have blue light filters baked in. I've heard of brands like Ocushield and Tech Armor, but I haven't personally tested them.

Invest in an eye-friendly monitor. If you're using a second screen (or considering an upgrade to your home office setup), look for monitors that are designed with eye care in mind. Features like flicker-free tech, low blue light modes, and anti-glare coatings are your friends. The BenQ Eye Care Series is a solid choice, and ASUS Eye Care monitors are pretty affordable. Look for products that are certified for eye health.

Work-Life Playbook

Résumé Highlights:

- Structure is everything. Whether you're managing a wildly chaotic puppy, a chronic illness, or a creative business, some kind of routine will keep you from spiraling into overwhelm.
- Remote work can be a lifeline, but only if you approach it intentionally. That means building your day around your energy, setting clear boundaries, and making rest an integral part of your plan.
- Just because you work from home doesn't mean you're "free." People may not get it—but you get to set the tone and expectations for how your time is treated.
- Flexibility is a tool, not an excuse to let the day unravel.
- Your schedule should serve you, not stress you out.

Power Moves:

- Create a basic "skeleton" schedule with a set start time, a clear break, and a stop time that helps signal the end of your workday.

- Choose a task tracker that works for you. Color code it, scribble it on a whiteboard, or voice-note it to yourself—just make sure it helps, not hinders.
- Identify your peak energy window and block that time for high-priority work. Treat it like gold.
- Batch similar work together to reduce brain-switching fatigue and give your brain a break.
- Define your work-start and work-stop rituals. Whether it's lighting a candle or shutting your laptop with a flourish, find your signals.

CEO Mindset Check-In:

- What time of day do you feel the sharpest mentally or physically?
- What parts of your workday drain you the most? Can you delegate or rearrange them?
- Have you communicated your work boundaries to the people around you, or are you hoping they just "get it"?
- Is your current work setup helping or hurting your health? What small change could improve it?
- Do you give yourself grace when your body doesn't cooperate, or do you double down on guilt and shame?

Chapter 8

The Freelance Freedom Double-Edged Sword

It was April 2019, and I stretched awake as my hungry hippo beagle bounced on her front paws next to me in bed. "Come on, Mom! Feed me!" But as I shifted, I realized I had my own pressing concerns. My hands and feet were riddled with painful pins and needles with patchy numbness. *That is a first*, I thought. Must have slept weird.

I rolled out of bed and started my usual routine, chugging coffee and stepping into a hot shower, waiting for the feeling to pass. It didn't. But canceling my plans wasn't even a thought. I had a big day planned.

I had a relatively new client and was scheduled to work in their office that day. It was a huge marketing agency about ninety minutes away. It was a contract that genuinely excited me. Cool clients, a fun team, and the chance to prove myself as a contractor who could handle busy agency-level work. No way was I going to bail on this.

I packed my lunch, my work bag, and got in the car. With eagerness, I started the engine, pushed in the clutch and brake—and instantly winced. (Yes, I was driving a stick shift!)

Not only was it painful to press the pedals due to the sensation of knitting-needle-sized pins and needles, but the patchy numbness made it hard to tell if I was pushing enough. A ninety-minute drive ahead, in traffic, with feet that weren't fully cooperating? I had to admit it was a dangerous situation.

I sat there, gripping the steering wheel, worrying my lip, trying to decide what to do. I hated canceling something so crucial to my business. What if this made me look unreliable? What if this contract fell apart before it even got started?

But in the end, I decided my safety, and the safety of everyone else on the road, were more important. I called my client, apologized profusely, and let them know I wouldn't be able to come in.

My client was incredibly understanding. Kind, even. I appreciated that more than she probably realized.

That moment was my first taste of the anguish that comes with juggling a jerk body and business. The brutal, gut-punch realization that no matter how much I wanted to push through, my body might have other plans.

At the time, I had no idea I had just entered the wacky world of chronic illness.

Fast-forward a couple of years, and I took in-office work entirely off the table. My body had become too unreliable, and I hated putting myself in the position of having to cancel. Instead of setting myself up for failure, I structured my business in a way that made sense for my reality.

If I never work in clients' offices, I will never have to disappoint them by canceling. Simple.

Of course, people still asked. Could I work in their office one day a week? A couple of times a month? It would be so much easier for collaboration. Saying "no" went from painfully uncomfortable to second nature. I never explained my health. I never launched into a monologue about nerve pain, numbness, or how my body had the unpredictability of a raccoon on an energy drink. Instead, I set boundaries without giving a personal medical backstory.

I'd say, "Because I'm a high-demand contractor, it's too difficult to commit to in-office workdays. Most of my clients work in social media, and social media is incredibly unpredictable. I would never want to be working in your office when another brand has an emergency that requires my attention. It wouldn't be fair to either of you."

No one ever pushed back. And they shouldn't, because it was the truth.

When it comes to advocating for yourself in your career, you don't have to justify your decisions with deeply personal reasons. You don't have to explain your health to people who have no business knowing it. You just need to set clear, professional boundaries that make sense. And if those boundaries also protect your health? Even better.

But I'm getting ahead of myself, aren't I? Let's find out if freelancing is the smart step for you.

Is Freelancing Right for You?

So, you're toying with the idea of joining the ranks of those who swap the 9-to-5 grind for the freedom of being their own boss.

But before you dive in, let's break down what freelancing really entails, the traits that make freelancers successful, and whether this path aligns with your personality and work style.

Freelancing is a significant segment of the workforce. In the United States, freelancers make up approximately 37 percent of the workforce, with around 59 million people engaged in freelance work. Projections suggest that by 2027, this number could increase to 86.5 million, accounting for more than half of the U.S. workforce.

Globally, an estimated 1.57 billion people were freelancing in 2024, representing about 47 percent of the working population. This shift screams, "It's workin' for me, so come join the party!" but is it really the right fit for us impaired health baddies? Let's look at some of the typical traits of successful freelancers.

- **Self-discipline:** Without a boss hovering over your shoulder, managing deadlines and staying productive requires a strong sense of discipline.
- **Networking skills:** Building and maintaining client relationships is crucial. Networking helps in finding new opportunities and sustaining a steady workflow.
- **Flexibility:** The ability to adapt to different projects, clients, and industries keeps freelancers relevant and in demand.
- **Financial acumen:** Managing irregular income, setting rates, and handling taxes necessitate a good grasp of financial matters.
- **Time management:** Juggling multiple projects requires effective time management to meet deadlines without compromising quality.

On the flipside, there are attributes that aren't so hot for gigsters.

- **Preference for structure:** If you thrive in environments with clear guidelines and consistent routines, the unpredictable nature of freelancing might be unsettling.
- **Aversion to risk:** Without the security of a steady paycheck and benefits, freelancing can be a financially unpredictable endeavor.
- **Discomfort with self-promotion:** Freelancers must market their skills and seek out opportunities, which can be daunting for those who are uncomfortable with self-promotion.
- **Struggling with self-management:** You must be very disciplined when working for yourself. There isn't anyone holding you accountable except you.

Still unsure if freelancing is the right fit? Answer these questions, tally up your score, and find out whether you're *Born to Be Free*, need *More Soul-Searching*, or if it's *Time to Explore Other Options*.

1. How do you feel about working without a boss looking over your shoulder?
A) Love it. I'm self-motivated and prefer making my own decisions. (1 point)
B) I like the idea, but I sometimes need a little external pressure to stay on track. (2 points)
C) Absolutely not. I need clear direction and structure, or I feel lost. (3 points)

2. How do you handle inconsistent income?

A) I'm okay with financial ups and downs as long as I have a plan. (1 point)

B) It stresses me out, but I think I could make it work with a safety net. (2 points)

C) Nope, I need a steady paycheck, or I won't sleep at night. (3 points)

3. How comfortable are you with self-promotion?

A) I can market myself and network with confidence when I have the spoons. (1 point)

B) I'll do it if I have to, but it's definitely not my favorite thing. (2 points)

C) If I have to sell myself, I'd rather just stay traditionally employed. (3 points)

4. What's your approach to deadlines?

A) I set my own deadlines and stick to them, no problem. (1 point)

B) I work best with external deadlines, but can manage my time if needed. (2 points)

C) Deadlines stress me out, and I need someone checking in to keep me accountable. (3 points)

5. How do you feel about handling the financial side of work? (Invoices, taxes, contracts, etc.)

A) I'm comfortable managing my own money and paperwork. (1 point)

B) I'll do it, but I might need help or software to keep it organized. (2 points)

C) That sounds like my personal nightmare. I prefer HR and payroll handling everything. (3 points)

6. When it comes to job security, you prefer…

A) Having multiple clients so I'm never dependent on one paycheck. (1 point)
B) Some stability but with the flexibility to try different things. (2 points)
C) A steady, predictable income and long-term job security. (3 points)

7. How do you feel about wearing multiple hats in your job?

A) Love it. I enjoy switching between projects and learning new skills. (1 point)
B) It's fine in small doses, but I like having some specialization. (2 points)
C) I'd rather stick to one role and become really good at it. (3 points)

8. What's your take on work-life integration?

A) I love the idea of setting my own hours and choosing when I work. (1 point)
B) I want flexibility, but I'm worried about work bleeding into my personal life. (2 points)
C) I like having clear boundaries between work and personal time. (3 points)

Results: Add Up Your Points

8-12 Points: Born to Be Free!

Do you hear that? Freelancing is calling your name! You thrive on independence, adaptability, and the idea of controlling your own work life. The unpredictability of freelancing excites you. Go forth, build that career, and make your own rules.

13-18 Points: More Soul-Searching Needed

You like the idea of freelancing, but there are a few areas that might be challenging. Maybe the inconsistent income worries you, or you're not in love with the idea of self-promotion. You might thrive with a portfolio career or a more traditional part-time job that is coupled with a part-time gig, a mix of freelancing and part-time, or contract work. Consider testing the waters before going all-in.

19-24 Points: Time to Explore Other Options

Freelancing may not be the best fit for you, at least not right now. You value stability, structure, and predictability, and that's okay! Traditional employment offers security that freelancing just can't. If you still want flexibility, look into remote jobs, hybrid work, or part-time roles. There's more than one way to build a sustainable career without jumping into full-time freelancing.

Freelancing is about working for yourself and knowing yourself. Whatever you choose, make sure it aligns with your skill set, personality, and goals.

What to Expect as a Freelancer

Embarking on a freelance career is thrilling and a little nerve-wracking, because it requires you to figure things out fast. The biggest shock for most newbies is the variable income. It certainly kept me up at night before I started my own business.

Unlike a traditional salaried job, where a paycheck magically appears in your bank account every two weeks, freelancing keeps you on your toes. Some months, you're rolling in invoices and feeling like a financial genius. Other months, you're eating peanut butter straight from the jar, questioning your life choices.

I also can't ignore the lack of traditional benefits. If you've spent your career in a full-time job, you probably took things like health insurance, retirement plans, and paid time off for granted. Freelancers? No benefits for you! No HR department, no sick days, no neatly packaged 401(k). Instead, you have to hunt down your own insurance, figure out retirement planning, and say so long to paid days off.

Enough doom and gloom, let's talk about the good stuff.

Autonomy. Freelancing hands you the keys to your own career. You choose your projects, set your schedule, and work from wherever you want. Your office can be a cozy corner of your living room, a beachside café, or your bed. I love working from my RV in a campground. No micromanaging boss. No passive-aggressive emails about office fridge etiquette.

I just sold myself on this life all over again!

Of course, all that freedom comes with a catch: responsibility. Every single aspect of your career—landing clients, sending invoices, chasing down late payments, marketing yourself, handling contracts, and, oh yeah, *doing the work,* falls on your shoulders. There's no IT department to fix your tech issues or a finance team to sort out your taxes. Just you, keeping everything afloat. Freelancing is the ultimate test in self-sufficiency, and if you're not ready to juggle multiple roles at once, it can get overwhelming fast.

One thing I struggle with as a freelancer is the ever-changing to-do list. Yes, many of my contracts have regular duties that are consistent throughout the month, but clients can also have urgent needs that require new work. It can throw a wrench in your well-planned day. Or completely turn your world upside down if you were taking a rest-and-reset health day.

What do you think? Is freelancing everything you hoped for, or putting you in an endless anxiety spiral? It depends on how well you handle unpredictability, independence, and a little bit of chaos. If you're up for the challenge, the freedom can be worth it. But if the idea of unstable income and managing your own benefits triggers a mast cell reaction, it might be worth reconsidering. Either way, knowing what to expect is half the battle. The other half? Figuring out if you're really ready to take the leap.

Build a Sustainable Freelance Career Without Burning Out

Freelancing sounds like freedom. You can set your own hours, pick your own clients, and work from the comfort of your bed in fuzzy socks. And it should come with a gigantic warning label: Freedom is only as good as the structure you build around it. Without clear boundaries, smart work habits, and an ironclad ability to manage expectations, your custom career can spiral from "spoon-smart success" to "never-ending chaos." There's no boss to save you from bad decisions, no onboarding to smooth out the learning curve, and no safety net if you oversell on your deliverables.

Rules can help you from running yourself into the ground. And don't worry, not the kind that stifles creativity, but the kind that keeps you from self-sabotage. These seven rules will help you work smarter so you don't crash and burn before your career even takes off.

The Seven Rules of Freelancing

1. Never lie about your skill set or experience. You might have applied for a traditional full-time job before and exaggerated a little on your resume, knowing you'd have onboarding training, coworkers to lean on, or a manager to guide you along the way. That safety net doesn't exist when you work for yourself. If you tell a client you know how to do something, you'd better know how to do it. There's no built-in mentorship, no structured training, and no one to pick up the slack when you overpromise and underdeliver. Your reputation is your resume, and if you fumble because you misrepresented yourself, word gets around fast.

2. Underpromise and overdeliver. I see far too many freelancers and business owners do the opposite. They make big promises to impress clients, then scramble to meet expectations they should have never set in the first place. Even as someone managing multiple autoimmune diseases and a connective tissue disorder, I always aim to deliver early. I build in extra buffer time for projects, knowing that my health can be unpredictable. If a client needs something by Friday, I set my personal deadline for that project for Wednesday. This means I'm either delivering early or right on time if the unexpected happens. This builds trust, makes clients more willing to accommodate your needs, and prevents unnecessary stress when the inevitable bad health days hit.

3. Never get comfortable with workplace gossip. This applies whether you're freelancing or working as an employee. Although a company may make you feel like family, remember that you are still an external contractor or an employee with limited job security. Avoid getting pulled into office drama. It never ends well, and when you're already advocating for yourself in other areas, the last thing you need is extra friction in workplace relationships.

4. Become a pro at documenting everything. Overcommunicating is better than undercommunicating. If you have a meeting about next month's workload, document every detail—what was discussed, who is responsible for what, when deliverables are due, and what expectations are. There are even AI tools that can record and recap meetings, as well as list next steps. Don't assume everyone is on the same page. If the client later claims a deadline was different from what you remember, you need written proof—an email, a project tracker, a shared document—so you can refer back and say, "Actually, we agreed on this date."

5. Always confirm the details. Just because a company has a project scheduled for June doesn't mean they want your work in June. You might assume May is a reasonable submission date, but unless you've confirmed that timeline, you could be way off. Instead of guessing, state it outright: "I can have this ready by May 15th—does that work for you?" Getting a direct answer eliminates confusion and prevents deadline disasters.

6. Repeat after me: "None-ya business." Should you disclose your chronic illness to clients or employers? I rarely do. Not because I'm ashamed, but because in most cases, it's irrelevant. If I can meet my deadlines and produce high-quality work, my health is not their concern.

In initial meetings, I don't say, "I have a chronic illness, so I may disappear for two weeks." Instead, I say, "I have a very tight schedule, but I'm excited to take on this work. Here's when I'll be available."

I let them know that I only take two Zoom meetings per month and that I do not travel for in-person work. If they say it doesn't work for them, I say, "Great, I wish you the best," and I move on.

This is setting expectations. It's making sure you don't sell a false bill of goods while also protecting your privacy and professional boundaries. You don't need to justify why you work the way you do. You just need to state your availability and let them decide if it's a fit.

7. Be confident, even if you have to fake it until you believe it. As a subcontractor, I was on a client call where someone else was presenting PowerPoint slides. Every slide, sometimes multiple times per slide, the person presenting would ask if the client had any changes, if they liked it, or if something didn't feel right. After hearing something like, "Are you sure this feels good? Do you need any changes?" over a dozen times, the client started offering suggestions—even when they weren't passionate about the changes.

The point I'm trying to make is that by repeatedly asking "Do you want edits?" the presenter opened the door to more work and undermined their own confidence in the process. By not standing firm in their choices, they allowed the client to feel like they had to make changes, even if they weren't needed. Asking once or twice if changes are required is totally professional and considerate, but avoid overdoing it.

Entrepreneurship is about being a good boss to yourself. You may be pleasantly surprised how those good vibes trickle down to your clients. That means setting clear expectations, documenting everything, and knowing when to say no. *Stick to these seven rules, and you'll be ahead of the game.*

Work-Life Playbook

Résumé Highlights

- Freelancing gives you flexibility, autonomy, and control, but only if you build it intentionally. Otherwise, it's just chaos with a nicer wardrobe.
- Saying "no" doesn't require a TED Talk about your diagnosis. Boundaries can be firm, respectful, and totally medical-history-free.
- Freelancing is a test in self-discipline, self-advocacy, and figuring out how to do five jobs in one while protecting your health.
- Without rules, freelancing can spiral from dreamy to disastrous.

Power Moves

- Set clear work boundaries *before* a flare forces you to. Don't agree to in-person meetings if your body isn't built for them—full stop.
- Practice delivering "no" responses professionally and without overexplaining. And always offer a positive

alternative. Say, "That's not something I offer, but here's what I'm happy to provide...."

■ Learn the seven freelancer survival rules. Print them. Live them. Tattoo them. (Disclaimer: I'm joking.).

CEO Mindset Check-In

■ What boundaries do you need to set (or re-set) with current or potential clients to protect your health and sanity?

■ What parts of freelancing feel empowering? What parts feel overwhelming, and what support would help?

■ Of the seven rules used to help avoid burnout, which one(s) will you struggle with the most? Which one(s) will you totally crush?

Chapter 9

Advocacy in Action: Working With Employers

It is what it is.

Maybe that phrase is helping you keep your current job. It's the reason you grin and bear it, the reason you collect that biweekly paycheck, the reason you tell yourself that even though your body is screaming for mercy, at least you have stability. It keeps your parents or partner off your back. It lets you sleep at night, even if only in that exhausted, resigned way that comes with knowing you're pushing yourself past your limits.

But let me tell you one absolute fact you can take from this book: saying, "It is what it is" will never get you where you want to go. It's not the mindset of someone building a flexible, sustainable career. It's not the rallying cry of a person advocating for themselves in a job that's wrecking them. It's a *blah* when you need a *rah-rah*.

Bring your favorite movie or book to mind. Picture the main character in a pivotal moment—one of those scenes where everything is on the line. Maybe it's Katniss leading a rebellion in *The Hunger Games*, or the remaining Avengers realizing they have to fight against impossible odds. Maybe it's the Red Wedding moment that shocked every *Game of Thrones* fan into horrified silence. Hold onto that feeling, that gasp, that *holy shit, what-happens-next* moment.

Now imagine that character shrugging and saying, *"Eh. It is what it is."* And then walking away.

Not exactly compelling storytelling, is it?

We don't watch heroes walk off the battlefield. We watch them fight, even when the odds are stacked against them. Even when they've failed before. Even when they're terrified and don't believe in themselves. You might not be dodging arrows or wielding a magic hammer, but make no mistake: *this* is your moment. This is when you decide whether you accept your circumstances or advocate for something better.

I had my own *it is what it is* moment. I found myself in one of the hardest situations of my freelance career, and I wanted to walk away from it.

I had spent years building up my expertise, only to find myself in a *perfect storm*. My initial set of clients had completed their contracts, and I wasn't pulling in enough new work to make up for it. I panicked.

Dear God, what have I done?

I had left the stability of a full-time job to build something of my own. I had taken the risk and put in the work. And now, it was slipping. At least, that's what I thought at the time.

While searching for contract or part-time work online, I came across a job listing that stopped me in my tracks. It was for a personal brand I followed on social media—someone whose story and mission I respected. The job was remote, the team was small, and best of all, it was all about animal and environmental advocacy. I had spent years in marketing. Now, I could use my experience to make a difference.

I didn't even hesitate. I applied immediately.

The application process should have been my first red flag. It was brutal—more than a dozen pages of writing assignments, multiple rounds of video interviews, and even creating a fully produced video (which I had never done before and wasn't part of the job description). But I was determined. I pushed aside the nagging feeling that something wasn't right. I got the offer. And I took it.

Cue the wind and rain.

Five months in, I was miserable. The job was nothing like it had been advertised. I had been thrown miles back in my career—no trust, no independence, micromanagement at a level that made my ass twitch. I was sitting in constant video meetings to discuss things as small as whether we *really* needed a folder labeled "Social Media Strategy" in Google Drive.

It was clear this wasn't a team. The founder of this company had rocketed to success through a book deal, a TED talk, a viral video, and now, an entire business built around maintaining that fame. And that individual? They did not trust anyone. Why would they? They had built something from scratch, convinced their way was the only way, and anyone who joined the company was expected to fall in line.

I found out later the turnover rate was horrific. People were coming in and out faster than customers at a Taco Bell on a Friday night.

And the worst part? The "cause" I had signed up for—animal and environmental advocacy—wasn't even a priority. It was a secondary thought at best, a marketing tool at worst. What really mattered were lead magnets, email capture, and product sales funnels.

I was crushed. I had ignored my gut during the interview process. I had jumped at the first sign of distress in my own business and thrown myself into something I wasn't meant for. And here's the kicker: the timing of my business slowdown? Completely normal! I would later learn that many freelancers experience a dip at the end of the year and during the holidays. I had panicked for no reason.

The director of operations at this company saw I was struggling. She recommended I work one-on-one with a leadership coach they had hired because—shocker!—I wasn't the only one having issues under this "influencer's" leadership.

That coach, let's call her Betty, brought the clarity.

Betty and I had a couple of discovery calls, where she introduced me to a simple but powerful concept: the difference between playing in the NFL and then suddenly returning to high school football.

She explained that I had played at the highest level—worked with top coaches and played with teammates who were at the same level of experience and skill. And now? It was like I was back at high school. The playbook didn't make sense. The coaching felt chaotic. The team wasn't in sync.

It wasn't about whether the team was good or bad. It was that I didn't belong there.

And the thunder rolled.

At the same time this was happening, my beloved beagle—the absolute heart of my life—was entering hospice. Sixteen years of companionship, my post-college depression lifeline, and my best friend. He still had some spunk left, but his body was failing him. And I was wasting my days working 12-hour shifts for a job that made me miserable.

I put in my notice.

The founder responded with, "Good, because I was going to fire you anyway."

A real classy broad!

Oh, but she also required me to stay for six weeks per my contract.

So, you were going to fire me, but you want me to stick around for six more weeks? Interesting.

I lasted four weeks.

I quit on a Friday. My sweet boy left us on Tuesday.

I took two weeks to mourn. I had some savings, which gave me that grace period. I abandoned my business. Had one of the worst job experiences of my life. And my soul was shredded at the loss of my baby.

I could have said, "It is what it is" for many more weeks and fallen deeper into depression. But that wasn't going to fix anything. So, I got back to work—networking, posting in Facebook Groups, reaching out to former clients and coworkers. I was terrified and lost, but I was pushing through.

Then I got a text. Someone was offering me nearly full-time freelance work…for another personal brand.

Every instinct screamed, "Oh, hell no!" But I challenged myself. Was I really going to let one bad experience define an entire industry?

I met with the potential employers over coffee and was upfront about my concerns. They were open, honest, and they ran their business well. Over time, I realized they weren't like my former employer. They were hardworking, smart, and creative.

More opportunities rolled in. I delivered ahead of schedule, exceeded expectations, and soon, I was invoicing five-figure months.

I reclaimed my voice. For months, I had let someone else dictate my worth, question my abilities, and make me feel like I wasn't capable of leading my own career. And if you've ever been in a job where your needs weren't respected, where your skills were doubted, or where you felt trapped because of health concerns, you know precisely how soul-crushing that can be.

You Can't Outsource Your Own Well-Being

Put this on repeat in your noggin: *no one is going to make change happen for you.* You have to do it for yourself. I learned the hard way that staying silent, swallowing my frustrations, and hoping things would magically improve was a recipe for burnout and disappointment. Most workplaces are designed for productivity, not employee well-being. While I have had intuitive and empathetic clients and managers who picked up on my needs, most people are too overwhelmed with their own lives and struggles to notice yours. You are in charge at the beginning, middle, and end of every day. It's uncomfortable to always take the initiative and sail your own ship, but constantly hoping someone is going to rescue you will likely leave you floating adrift in a sea of resentment and exhaustion. Advocating for yourself at work—whether that means negotiating flexibility, setting boundaries, or leaving a situation that's actively hurting you—will ensure your survival.

So how do you do it? How do you communicate your needs without feeling like you're about to be labeled "difficult?" How do you push back against policies that make your job harder without risking your entire paycheck? And how do you start trusting yourself again when a bad job or employer has chipped away at your confidence? Let's break it down.

Communicate Your Needs With Confidence

Advocating for yourself in a professional setting can feel like walking a tightrope with orthostatic issues. You want to set clear boundaries, protect your health, and ensure that your work remains sustainable, but at the same time, you don't want to risk being seen as difficult, unreliable, or too much trouble. Whether you're freelancing, running a portfolio career, or working within a more traditional employer-employee setup, communicating your needs effectively is a major part of maintaining both your career and your well-being.

One of the biggest challenges in advocating for yourself at work is figuring out how much to disclose. While some people feel comfortable being completely open about their chronic illness, others prefer to keep it private. You don't owe anyone your full medical history. If you're freelancing or running your own business, clients don't need to know *why* you have limited availability—they just need to know what your availability is.

I learned this firsthand when I transitioned from traditional employment to freelancing. There's a certain level of safety in a full-time job. You likely have HR departments, legal protections, and (in some cases) medical leave options. But when you're self-employed, you are your HR department. You set your own policies. That means setting boundaries and expectations from the start, not waiting until a crisis forces you to explain why you suddenly can't meet a deadline.

Eight Tips on Advocacy in the Workplace

To handle advocacy in the workplace with extra care, I enlisted the help of Becca. She's a psychotherapist, a fellow Ehlers-Danlos Syndrome warrior, and someone who's had to navigate these same choppy waters in both her professional life and health journey. Becca started having symptoms as a kid—headaches, TMJ pain, joints doing their best impression of overcooked spaghetti. Like so many of us, she pinballed through doctors until she finally landed a diagnosis at twenty-four years old. She's now in her thirties, balancing her own chronic illness while helping others navigate theirs.

Becca gets it—both as a patient and as a professional who sees clients grappling with the messiness of chronic illness in the workplace. She went into grad school with eyes wide open. She knew a 32-hour workweek was her sweet spot, and that mornings were not her friend. This meant she'd have to advocate for herself early and often. She learned, the hard way, that a "disability accommodations" form shoved at a professor or employer is not a magical ticket to their understanding. And she knows that in the workplace, being curious instead of combative, and prepared instead of reactive, is how to increase the success of getting what you need.

So, let's get into Becca's advocacy advice for the workplace or with clients. These tactics can come in handy whether you're asking for accommodations, setting expectations, or just trying not to get steamrolled by someone who doesn't get it.

Here's the scoop, straight from Becca:

1. Advocacy starts before day one. Don't wait until you're drowning in a new job or client work to start talking about your needs or setting boundaries. If you know you need a 32-hour work week, say that up front or only accept a contract or job that aligns with that need. If mornings are a disaster for your body, ask for later shifts or declare your available work hours up front. Don't wait for the train wreck—plan ahead. As Becca put it: "We're more likely to have success if we know what we need for ourselves."

2. Curiosity beats combativeness. Yes, you have legal rights. Yes, it's frustrating when people don't get it. But storming in with "ADA says you have to!" is not the best approach and vibe. Instead, Becca suggests having a script ready. This may start off sounding like, "I'm not sure if you're aware, but…" or "Thank you for letting me know. I'm wondering if…" Approach it like you're inviting them to the table, not throwing the table at them.

3. Prepare for people to forget. If your illness is invisible (and, let's be honest, even if it isn't), people will often forget the guidelines you established. Becca reminds us that it isn't about them not caring; it's just human nature. Have your reminders ready: "Oh, hey, just a reminder, I need to sit sometimes because of my health issues." Be ready to say it again, and again, and again. It sucks, but it's the reality.

4. Focus on specifics. Vague requests like "I need flexibility" make people nervous. Concrete asks like, "I need a later start time but I'm happy to stay late," or "I need a specific type of mouse with my laptop" are easier for people to understand and approve.

5. Consider the culture. Becca points out that some industries may be more accommodating than others. While some workplaces can be more understanding of chronic illness, others may be met with some resistance to advocating. This is why it's important to consider culture when looking at companies or clients. We want to see that support is built into the culture, because we don't want to spend our spoons constantly fighting for appropriate accommodations.

6. Have your support system ready. Vent to your people. You need a place where you can say, "It's freaking bullshit that I have to do this again," so you can recharge and keep showing up with your game face.

7. Rehearsed statements are your secret weapon. Practice what you'll say before the conversation. Have a few options ready so you're not caught off guard. This may sound like, "I'd be happy to have a brainstorming meeting. As a reminder, I take video meetings on Tuesdays and Thursdays. Which day works for you?" It's emotional labor, yes, but as Becca says, "It's usually worth it in these kinds of situations."

8. Be realistic, not resigned. It's not fair that we have to advocate so hard. But waiting for people to read our minds or magically remember our needs? That's a recipe for burnout. Becca says it best: "It's a lot of work, and it sucks, but if we expect that we can just show up somewhere and get what we need, we're going to be disappointed more often than not."

This area of advocacy is all about knowing the system you're walking into, the culture of the place, and having a proactive approach. It's also about giving yourself grace when you have to fight the same damn battle again because people will forget. Not because they don't care, but because they're busy starring in the movie of their own lives.

At the end of the day, advocating for yourself in your career is about ensuring you don't set yourself up for a letdown. Whether you're freelancing, juggling multiple gigs, or working a more traditional job, you're the one responsible for setting boundaries that allow you to keep working sustainably. Clients and employers will take as much as you give. It's up to you to make sure you're not giving too much.

For extra support, you may want to explore these resources:

- **Chronic Disease Coalition:** They have ambassadors across the United States, ways to get involved in advocacy, and educational materials.
- **Job Accommodation Network (JAN):** Offers practical solutions for supporting chronically ill employees through workplace accommodations.
- **Disability Management Employer Coalition (DMEC):** Provides education, tools, and resources to optimize workforce productivity and maintain compliant absence and disability programs.
- **Chronically Capable:** They work to remove the fear and stigma of living with chronic illness or disability from the hiring process.
- **The EPIC Foundation:** They provide support, advocacy, and tools to those affected by chronic illnesses.

Work-Life Playbook

Résumé Highlights

- "It is what it is" is not a life strategy. It's a big 'ol warning that you may be betraying your own needs.
- You don't owe anyone your medical history to justify a boundary. You need to know what works for you and how to effectively communicate that.
- A toxic job can make you question your worth, but surviving it means you've already proven your strength.
- Preparation beats panic. Knowing your needs ahead of time makes it easier to communicate them without spiraling.
- Advocacy done right is a power move, not a pity plea. It protects your energy, your work, and your future.

Power Moves

- Write out three "non-negotiables" you need in a work environment before you apply to another job or say "yes" to a new client.
- Draft a go-to script for boundary setting (something like, "I'm happy to take video meetings on Tuesdays and Thursdays—what works for you?").
- Make a list of physical accommodations you might need (chair, mouse, schedule changes). Use Becca's advice: specifics are easier to say "yes" to.
- Practice reframing. Instead of "They should already know this," try, "They may have forgotten, so I'll remind them with grace."

- Audit your current work environment. Are you being underestimated or overlooked? That's not something you have to tolerate.
- Save a vent space. Whether it's a Facebook group, a therapist, or a spoonie friend, have a designated outlet so you can release, then reset.

CEO Mindset Check-In

- Where in your life are you still saying, "It is what it is" when what you mean is, "This isn't working"?
- Have you been waiting until things are bad enough to advocate for yourself?
- What boundary have you failed to set because you were scared of being labeled difficult?
- Who benefits when you stay quiet? (Hint: it's probably not you.)
- What would it look like to show up curious instead of combative in your next tough conversation?
- Are you building a career that respects your reality, or one that demands you ignore it?

Chapter 10

Face Setbacks with Grace

"I've never seen lightning so close!"

That was my last thought before blinding, hot light filled my car. Then the air felt oddly still and heavy. My windshield wipers stopped. Other vehicles moved past me, but my car wasn't responding. I pressed my foot to the gas. Nothing. I yanked the steering wheel, but it felt like it was stuck in cement. Smoke poured through the vents, bringing with it the creeping realization that this wasn't just an electrical glitch.

My car had been freakin' struck by lightning.

I gripped the stiff steering wheel, using what little momentum I had to veer onto the shoulder. When I reached for my phone, raindrops carried tiny shards of broken glass down my arms. Both driver's side windows were shattered, as well as the back window. The storm was still raging, and my car was filling with smoke. Getting out seemed dangerous, but staying put didn't feel much better. I scrambled into the back seat, where the air was clearer, and dialed the one number no one ever wants to call.

"This is 911. What is your emergency?"

"I've been struck by lightning!" I shouted over the roar of the rain and wind. "I'm on Route 44 by the airport." Thunder crashed through my sentence, swallowing my words.

The operator kept asking for my location, but the storm was too thick for me to see any landmarks. I wasn't even sure what to ask for first. Was my car going to explode? Was I in more danger staying inside or stepping out into a lightning storm?

"My car is on fire! Do I stay in the back seat or go outside?"

"I'm sorry, ma'am, I can't make that decision for you," he said.

I'd just been electrocuted by nature, and now I was dealing with legal protocols. Fantastic.

A minute later, sirens cut through the storm. A fire truck pulled up beside me, and a firefighter pulled open the back door and escorted me to the back of his fire truck. His expression was disturbingly calm as he asked if I was okay and handed me a form to fill out.

"Does this happen all the time?" I asked.

"Yeah, happens all the time." He looked at me like I had a couple of nuts loose.

The fact that cars are often struck by lightning while in motion was news to me. News I wished I'd heard secondhand.

I stared at the paperwork, trying to process the absurdity of the situation. The form kept asking for details about the other car involved in the accident.

"I don't know how to fill this out," I said.

"What kind of vehicle hit you?"

"God?"

He stared and blinked. I realized the disconnect.

"Sir, I was struck by lightning."

Every firefighter within earshot whipped their heads in my direction. Their eyes widened, and just like that, everything shifted. One grabbed a flashlight, the other asked about dizziness, pain, or disorientation. Finally, someone was reacting with the appropriate amount of shock.

By the time they finished their assessment, the storm had passed. The firemen walked me back to my car and pointed to a cigarette-sized burn in the roof where the lightning had entered. The bolt had traveled along the driver's side doors and exited through my front tire. I stared at the now-flat rubber, still trying to process that I had just been inside a car while actual lightning shot through it.

I was lucky. Completely unharmed. My vehicle was another story—my insurance company declared it was totaled.

That day became one hell of a story. But not all plot twists are that simple. Some take something from you—something you depended on. A job. A sense of security. Your car. And when that happens, it can be a weird, unsettling detour.

Losing a job might feel like a test, something you have to push through until you find the next opportunity. A business struggling to survive could be a trial, something that takes work and strategy to course-correct. But then there are the plot twists that rip the ground out from under you, the ones that rewrite your story completely, whether you're ready or not.

Plot twists are unavoidable, friends. Whether it's an injury, an illness, a layoff, or an unexpected detour, they will happen. You can't always see them coming, and you definitely don't always get a say in it. But you do get to decide what happens next.

Sometimes, you find another way to reach your goal. Sometimes, you pivot to something new. Sometimes, you stop running down a path that was always meant to be a dead end.

And sometimes, when the storm clears, you realize that the life you're building now—the one that exists after the plot twist—is better than the one you thought you lost.

When Your Body Betrays the Plan

As we all know, when the body betrays the plan, it doesn't send a courtesy email. No calendar invite. No heads-up that things are about to go bananas. One day, you're doing your job, feeling like you're making progress, and the next, your body gets struck by metaphorical lightning. And not in a "take a nap and feel better" kind of way. More like a "welcome to your new reality, hope you weren't too attached to that old life" kind of way.

I had one of those moments when I was offered a leadership role at a hot, up-and-coming marketing agency. It was the kind of opportunity most people never get. I didn't have to interview. I got to write my own job description, outlining not just what I wanted to do, but also what I didn't want to do—like travel for in-person meetings or get stuck managing a team full of chaos gremlins.

On paper, it was the dream gig. A role that aligned with my skill set, my talents, and a chance at mentoring young marketing professionals. I could work with amazing brands, create top-tier social media content, and build something really gosh darn cool. If I had been offered this job before I got sick, I wouldn't have even thought twice. I would have jumped in headfirst, probably sending back my signed offer letter within 30 seconds.

But I was sick. Life was different now.

I had already been contracting with this agency for a few months, and my body was not-so-subtly telling me that working more hours and taking on more stress was coming at a price. The fatigue got worse. My joints felt like they were hosting their own personal bonfire. The brain fog gave me a puzzled Elmer Fudd face. My dry eye and vision issues became so bad that there were times I couldn't even decipher words in an email.

I knew exactly how this story would end if I took the job. I'd work myself into the ground trying to prove I could handle it. I'd push through, ignore the warning signs, and then inevitably crash. The kind of impact that would force me to quit anyway. And in the process, I'd be letting down an employer I respected and a team I wanted to do right by.

So I turned it down.

That's the kind of decision you have to make when your body insists on having a seat at the HR table. It wasn't just me deciding what was best for my career. It was me, my inappropriate immune response, and my faulty connective tissue sitting together in a tense boardroom, all casting votes on whether I could take this job or not. And in the end, the body outvoted the ambition.

These are the tough choices we have to make when our health is not a predictable variable in the career equation. Sometimes, it's not a matter of if we can do something, but for how long before it wrecks us completely.

If you've ever had to walk away from an opportunity because your body simply wouldn't allow it, you know exactly how gut-wrenching that decision is. You wonder if you're making the right call, if maybe you could have handled it. You sit with the "what ifs" and the frustration of knowing that you are capable, but your body simply refuses to cooperate.

But listen up, my busted buddies: Turning down something that would destroy you is an act of self-preservation.

So what happens next? What do you do when your body forces a career pivot you didn't see coming or one you've been dreading for a while?

First, let yourself grieve. Seriously. Losing the ability to do the work you once loved, or even just tolerated because it paid the bills, is a loss. You don't have to pretend it's fine. You don't have to jump straight into a silver-lining "everything happens for a reason" mindset. Sit with the frustration. Let yourself be mad, upset, disappointed. Because once you process those feelings, you'll have a lot more mental energy to figure out what comes next.

Next, reassess what's possible. Just because one career path isn't sustainable anymore doesn't mean work itself is off the table. It just means you need to adapt. Maybe that means shifting to part-time or remote work instead of full-time. Perhaps it means leaving behind a physically demanding job in favor of something more flexible. Or it could mean diving into freelancing or starting a small business that allows you to work to the best of your ability.

Start by asking yourself some key questions:

- What parts of my job are the hardest on my body?
- Are there ways to modify my current work to make it more manageable?
- If I had to rebuild my career from scratch, what would I want it to look like?
- What skills do I already have that could translate into something more flexible?

The goal is to find a work setup that doesn't leave you in a permanent state of survival mode.

And lastly, build your safety net. If your body is unpredictable, your finances need to be as stable as possible. That might mean applying for short-term disability if you qualify, looking into assistance programs, or making sure you have multiple income streams so you're never relying on just one source. Even something as simple as having a small emergency fund for when things go south can make a huge difference.

Your career will have pivots. That's inevitable. But the pivots don't have to be the end of everything. They are a redirection. They can lead to a work life that makes sense for the body you have today—not the one you had before you got sick, and not the one you wish you had.

Because when the body betrays the plan, the only real option is to rewrite the plan. And while that might not be the story you wanted to tell, it doesn't mean it won't be a damn good one.

Plot Twists that Throw Your Career for a Loop

In 2020, while I was beginning to write this book, the world was in chaos. COVID-19 had shut down businesses, forced people into their homes, and turned toilet paper into a form of currency. People were losing jobs, losing loved ones, losing any sense of normalcy they once had.

And in the middle of all of that, I lost 60 percent of my income in two months.

I had been freelancing for years, building up a stable business, making smart decisions, and then—bam!—just like that, I was back to square one. Clients put projects on hold. Contracts were canceled. The work that had once been steady suddenly dried up. I took some solace in that it wasn't personal. Businesses everywhere were cutting back, holding onto whatever money they could, and independent contractors were the first to go.

With a sudden surplus of time and a rapidly dwindling bank account, I found myself staring at the unfinished draft of this book. The irony was almost too much. A book about finding success was sitting half-finished while I was trying to figure out how to recover from a major career setback.

I could have sat there thinking, I wish I had finished this book last year. I could have convinced myself it was too late, that the moment had passed. I could have worried about whether I even had the energy to pick it back up. Instead, I took action. I entered a contest for a free writing coach. I signed up for a ninety-nine-dollar nonfiction book-writing course. I stopped overthinking and started doing any little thing that felt like it moved the needle. I also met new people and forged new business connections.

Two months later, my business was back to where it had been before the pandemic. By the end of the year, I had doubled my income. I made more that year than I had in my entire career.

Career plot twists can definitely throw you off course, but sometimes they push you to build something even better than before. Don't get me wrong, I'll be the first to admit not every plot twist has a happy ending. It can force you to make impossible decisions or question whether you even have what it takes to keep going. Whether it's a business failing, an unexpected job loss, or a major financial setback, career disruptions can feel overwhelming and even impossible to recover from.

But I like to remember that every career, every business, every person who has ever built something worthwhile has dealt with seriously gnarly setbacks. The difference between the people who make it and the people who don't isn't luck or talent or having some magic formula for success. It's the ability to adapt, to pivot, to keep going even when everything feels like it's falling apart.

When you're starting a new business or making a career change, setbacks are inevitable. You will have clients ghost you. You will have months where money is tighter than you'd like. You will have moments where you wonder if you've made a colossal mistake.

The first step in dealing with setbacks is recognizing that they aren't personal. It isn't proof that you aren't good enough or that you should quit. It is part of the process. Every successful business owner, freelancer, and career changer has dealt with failure in some form. The ones who succeed are the ones who push through it.

One of the biggest setbacks people face is financial instability. Whether you're starting a business or shifting careers, there will almost always be a period where money is inconsistent. The mistake people make is assuming that means they've failed. It doesn't. It means you're in the messy middle— the part where things are still taking shape.

The best way to handle financial uncertainty is to plan for it. If you're making a career shift, start saving before you take the leap. If you're freelancing, set up multiple income streams to reduce your reliance on a single client. If you're starting a business, keep your expenses low while you're building. Stability doesn't come overnight, but with a plan, you can ride out the uncertain months without panicking.

Another common setback is slow progress. We live in a world where people expect instant success. If you don't have a profitable business in six months, people start asking if it's really worth it. If you don't land your dream job right away, it's easy to wonder if you made the wrong choice. But most overnight success stories are complete nonsense. Businesses take time to grow. Career shifts take time to pay off. The key is to keep going, even when it feels like nothing is happening.

Then there are the mental setbacks—the self-doubt, the imposter syndrome, the voice in your head that tells you you're not good enough, smart enough, or experienced enough to pull this off. That voice is a lying liar! And if you listen to it, you will talk yourself out of opportunities before you even give yourself a chance.

The only way to quiet that voice is through *action*. Keep moving forward, even if you're not sure it will work. Keep applying, keep reaching out, keep learning. You regroup. You reassess. You make a new plan.

Here are some affirmations to get you through the grittier moments. I included some for every mood, because if you're like me, there's a rainbow of moody moments.

Affirmations to Keep You Going Forward

- I have survived every bad day so far, and today is no different.
- Setbacks are detours, not dead ends.
- I am capable of success, even if my path looks different from what I planned.
- I am not behind. I am on my own timeline.
- Progress is still progress, even if it's slower than I wanted.

- I am not my productivity. I am valuable even when I need to rest.
- Resting is part of the process, not a failure.
- My worth is not measured by how many hours I work or how much I earn.
- I am creative, adaptable, and capable of figuring this out.
- I have permission to change the plan if it no longer works for me.

For When You Feel Snarky

- This setback is temporary. My stubbornness is forever.
- If my body wants to throw a tantrum, fine, but I'm still calling the shots.
- Today's disaster is just tomorrow's ridiculous story.
- If life wants to keep throwing plot twists, I demand a higher budget and better writers.
- I didn't come this far just to be taken down by a bad day and some questionable joints.
- If I have to choose between giving up and adjusting, guess what? I'm adjusting. Again.
- My career doesn't have to look normal, because, let's be real, nothing about my life is normal.
- I've reinvented myself before, and I'll do it again. Watch me.

For When You Need to Be Reminded You're Still a Badass

- I have built a life before, and I can build a new one.
- I have more strength than this setback.
- My dreams are still possible, even if the timeline has changed.
- I am not failing. I am evolving.
- I am allowed to succeed in unconventional ways.

- I am resilient, resourceful, and a force to be reckoned with.
- No setback is bigger than my ability to adapt.
- Every challenge I've faced has made me stronger. This one is no different.
- My story is still being written, and I decide how it goes.

Some days call for determination, some call for sarcasm, and some call for pure survival mode mantras. Whatever kind of setback you're facing, there's an affirmation here for you.

The Last Line of Defense: When Working Is Impossible

This book is about staying in the workforce, but sometimes, despite your best efforts, you need a financial safety net. If your health reaches a point where working is no longer possible, it's important to know your options.

- Short-Term and Long-Term Disability Insurance: If you're still employed, check if your employer offers disability insurance. If not, private plans exist, though they can be pricey. The best time to apply is before you desperately need it.
- Social Security Disability Insurance (SSDI) & Supplemental Security Income (SSI): While the application process is painfully slow and frustrating, these programs exist for those who are unable to work at all. If you need them, use them. Many chronic illness patients get denied on their first attempt, so working with a disability advocate or lawyer can help.
- Guaranteed Basic Income (GBI) Programs: Some cities and states are experimenting with basic income programs for people with disabilities or low-income workers. These programs provide monthly payments without work requirements to help cover living expenses.

- Food Assistance & Rent Relief: Many states have food assistance programs like SNAP, and some cities have short-term rent relief programs for those dealing with medical-related job loss. Even if you don't think you qualify, it's worth checking.

Work-Life Playbook

Résumé Highlights

- Plot twists are inevitable and can be career-ending flares, surprise layoffs, or a new diagnosis that reroutes everything.
- You don't need to white-knuckle your way through career detours. Your security blanket is a solid backup plan, a realistic budget, and maybe a fire extinguisher.

Power Moves

- Grieve the old plan. Journal it out. Cry in the shower. Blast some Alanis Morissette. Just don't skip this step. Grief ignored can become a tiresome weight to carry.
- Make a "plot twist prep kit." This includes an emergency fund goal, an updated resume, a list of side hustle ideas, and a reminder that you are more than your current title.
- Create your own permission slip: "I don't need to wait until everything crashes to change course. I can pivot now, protect my peace, and still be successful."

CEO Mindset Check-In

- What recent plot twist have you tried to push through instead of adapting to?

- What are you afraid will happen if you walk away from something that no longer fits?
- What strengths or skills do I have that could support a pivot, even if I haven't used them lately?

Chapter 11

The Unavoidable Money Talk

Chronic illness can suck the green right out of your wallet. Between medical bills, insurance fights, and prescriptions with price tags that make you scream in the middle of the pharmacy, money feels like a toddler constantly pulling at your pant leg.

I've had to make peace with the fact that my benefits package will probably never look like it did when I worked full-time, but that doesn't mean I don't find ways to make things work.

I don't take vacations. It's just not practical when you're living on a budget. My husband and I still have secondhand furniture. Cars are driven until they are no longer affordable to fix. As I'm writing this, both of our cars have over 155,000 miles, and I swear one of them is held together by sheer willpower. But that helps me afford to work part-time. We make sacrifices. And honestly? I don't miss most of those things. But every once in a while, something pops up that I don't want to cut corners on.

One day in late November, while setting up the Christmas tree, I realized I would soon need extra money for presents. I had budgeted for the basics, but the holiday season has a way of sneaking up on you with additional expenses. I stared at my bank account, then at my list of people for whom I wanted to get gifts, then back at my bank account. The math wasn't mathing. So, I got creative.

I turned to social media and offered watercolor pet portraits as custom holiday gifts. I figured there had to be pet lovers out there who'd love a painting of their furry friend under the Christmas tree. I also bought a bunch of small wooden discs, painted tiny Christmas trees and wreaths on them, drilled a hole in the top, threaded some twine through, and called them ornaments. They were simple. Easy. No one was going to call the Louvre about them, but they were cute enough to sell.

I made over $1,500 before the end of the year. (You can't see me, but I'm fist pumping with a paint brush in my hand.)

Before you start thinking, *Well, I'm not artistic, so that wouldn't work for me,* let me stop you right there. I wasn't a professional pet portrait artist when I started. I learned by watching two dozen YouTube tutorials. Yes, I had some art skills, but I wasn't an expert. I figured it out because I wanted to. And those little wooden ornaments? That required exactly zero artistic talent. They were tiny Christmas trees and wreaths.

What that holiday side hustle really taught me (besides how to efficiently paint a pittie's face in less than six hours) was how flexible a portfolio career could be. One month, I was primarily working as a copywriter. Next month I was running major social media campaigns. Another, I was making art for pet lovers. At different points in my career, I've juggled freelance projects, consulting gigs, and creative side hustles to piece together an income that worked with my body and interests. I realized that my financial security didn't have to come from one single job. It could come from a mix of skills, side gigs, and creative problem-solving.

If you're reading this and thinking, *I don't have any special skills to monetize,* I want you to light that thought on fire and allow the wind to carry the ashes away. You do. You just might not see them yet. If I hadn't taken a chance on my art skills, I wouldn't have had an extra $1,500 that Christmas. And if I hadn't tested different career ideas over time, I wouldn't have found a way to keep earning money without running myself into the ground.

Getting creative with your finances is equal parts about making money while spending less where you can. It may mean making smarter choices with medical expenses and figuring out where you can cut back without sacrificing the things that bring you joy.

One of the biggest financial game-changers for me was learning how to scrutinize my medical bills before blindly paying them. Did you know that almost 80 percent of medical bills contain errors? That means there's a very good chance you've been overcharged at some point and didn't even realize it. I make it a rule to never pay a medical bill until I've seen an itemized statement. I compare it to my insurance's explanation of benefits, make sure I was charged correctly, and call to dispute anything that looks suspicious. It's annoying, yes, but I'd rather spend fifteen minutes on hold than fork over an extra couple of hundred dollars I don't actually owe.

I also had to learn how to budget realistically for an unpredictable income. When you're working full-time, you have a steady paycheck. You know what's coming in every two weeks. When you're freelancing or juggling multiple income streams, your pay fluctuates, and that makes budgeting tricky. I figured out that instead of basing my budget on my highest-earning months, I had to base it on my lowest. That way, if I had a slow work month, I wasn't scrambling. And if I had a good month? Extra savings, baby!

I also had to get real about where my money was going. A couple of years ago, I sat down and went through every single subscription and recurring expense I had. It was horrifying. I was paying for apps I hadn't opened in months, streaming services I had forgotten I signed up for, and memberships I didn't need. Canceling those alone saved me close to $400 a year.

One year I saved myself $500 by shopping around for my MRI instead of just getting it where my doctor sent me.

So, if you're staring at your bank account wondering how you're supposed to make your new career path work, take a breath. Then take a look at your skills. Your spending. Your medical bills. Find one thing you can change today—whether it's testing out a side hustle, canceling an unnecessary expense, or calling your insurance company to dispute a bill. Start small. Adjust as you go.

Spoon-Sized Financial FAQs

I don't know about you, but talking about finances zaps my spoons faster than an autoimmune warrior in a heat wave. I'm quite certain I'm allergic to numbers. It's like mast cells have attacked that part of my brain. For the sake of my brain and yours, let's start small for this chapter.

I definitely had to phone a friend for this topic. I reached out to my buddy Jonathan Greeson. He is a financial planner who lives with Spinal Muscular Atrophy (SMA). He's a certified financial planner and Series 65 licensed advisor who provided some fast facts for us.

This is a lightning round of finance truths for freelancers, entrepreneurs, and chronically ill career shifters…especially if spreadsheets give you a rash.

Q: What's one financial red flag people overlook when leaving a full-time job?

A: Living paycheck to paycheck. Inconsistent income will only make it more stressful.

Q: What's the biggest financial mistake you see new entrepreneurs or freelancers make?

A: Buying equipment at the end of the year just to get a write-off.

Pro tip: Put that money in a retirement account instead. It can also be deductible.

Q: When do you need to set up an LLC instead of just operating as a sole prop?

A: If you have nothing, you're probably fine. People sue when there's money.

Pro tip: It's worth talking to a CPA or financial advisor before you grow.

Q: What's the first thing you'd do if you could only invest $100 a month?

A: Build an emergency cash fund. That's your foundation.

Q: What's one thing you wish more disabled freelancers knew about business expenses?
A: If something doesn't keep you alive or grow your business, don't buy it.

Q: What's your go-to mindset for spending money on support services or tools?
A: Wealthy people have assistants for everything. So I can too.

Q: Favorite way to track your business finances?
A: I use an app like Mint or QuickBooks, but I still track everything in Excel.

Q: What's something you wish you'd done differently in your early career?
A: I wish I had charged more.

Q: What is the most misunderstood part of financial planning for disabled people?
A: Understanding what assistance programs may be available and how they interact with income.

Fund Your Career Shift: Business Grants, Loans, and Training Resources

The fear of losing a steady paycheck, employer benefits, or job security can make these career shifts feel impossible. But hold on to the fact that there are financial resources, programs, and strategies that can help bridge the gap while you build a sustainable career that fits your health needs.

Next to managing health systems, managing your finances through a career transition can be as triggering as a little sunshine is to lupus.

If you're starting a business, diving into freelancing, or working multiple gigs, the financial uncertainty at the beginning can be overwhelming. While traditional loans aren't always accessible, some specific grants and programs can help cover startup costs, provide mentorship, and even fund equipment or training.

- State Vocational Rehabilitation (VR) services: Many states offer VR programs that help disabled or chronically ill individuals launch their own businesses, fund professional training, or secure accommodations for remote work. Even if you don't qualify as "disabled" in the traditional sense, these programs often support those who have medical conditions impacting long-term employment.
- Small Business Administration (SBA) grants and loans: The SBA provides resources, low-interest loans, and grants for entrepreneurs. Some programs are specifically designed for women, minorities, and people with disabilities. If you're looking to start a small business but don't have the capital, this is worth exploring.
- PASS (Plan to Achieve Self-Support) through Social Security: If you're on or near the eligibility line for SSI benefits but want to transition into self-employment, PASS lets you set aside money for business expenses without losing eligibility for certain benefits.
- Women's Business Centers (WBCs) and Chamber of Commerce support: These organizations provide free mentorship, business planning assistance, and funding

opportunities for entrepreneurs. Whether you need help setting up an LLC, marketing your business, or finding funding, WBCs and local business networks are an invaluable resource.

■ Freelancers Union and gig economy resources: If you're freelancing or juggling multiple income streams, organizations like the Freelancers Union provide legal protections, financial advice, and even access to affordable insurance plans.

If you're transitioning away from traditional employment, these programs can help you land on solid ground without burning through savings or taking on debt.

Make Work More Sustainable: Financial Safety Nets While You Build Stability

Even with the best planning, there are slow months, unexpected expenses, and flare-ups that make consistent income feel like a moving target. Instead of riding the feast-or-famine rollercoaster, use these programs to keep things steady while you get your career where it needs to be.

■ Medicaid buy-in for workers with disabilities: Many states allow people with chronic illnesses to keep Medicaid coverage while working by paying a small premium. This means you don't have to stay in a full-time job just to keep health insurance.

■ ABLE accounts (Achieving a Better Life Experience): If you developed your condition before age forty-six, you can use an ABLE account to save money without affecting benefits like Medicaid or SSI. This is a game-changer for anyone worried about long-term financial security while still working.

- Tax deductions for work-related disability expenses: The IRS allows for deductions on things like assistive technology, home office adaptations, and medical-related work expenses. If you need special equipment, a modified work setup, or even a virtual assistant to help with tasks, you may be able to write it off.

- Energy assistance and utility discounts: Many states offer discounted utility rates, grants for home modifications, and heating/cooling assistance for people with medical conditions. If you work from home, keeping your workspace comfortable year-round is a legitimate work expense.

- Crowdfunding and community support: While not ideal for long-term sustainability, mutual aid networks, community grants, and crowdfunding platforms (like GoFundMe or Give InKind) can help with unexpected medical bills or career shifts that require an upfront investment. Some chronic illness groups even have dedicated emergency relief funds for members.

Help to Reduce Your Healthcare Costs

The soaring costs of insurance premiums, medications, and medical services can make it seem impossible to maintain your health without draining your bank account. But before you resign yourself to a diet of ramen noodles and stress, let's explore some strategies to help you lower healthcare expenses and keep your financial goals within reach.

Understand and Review Your Medical Bills

Medical bills often read like a foreign language—confusing, jargon-filled, and seemingly designed to empty your wallet. Alarmingly, nearly 80 percent of medical bills contain errors. So, if you've ever looked at a bill and thought, "There's no way that's right," you might be onto something. Here's how to tackle the labyrinth:

- Examine your Explanation of Benefits (EOB): This document from your insurance company outlines what was charged, what they covered, and what you owe. Ensure the services listed match your actual treatments and that you're not being billed for services you didn't receive.
- Spot common billing mistakes: Look out for duplicate charges, services you didn't receive, or charges at out-of-network rates when you used in-network providers. Upcoding (billing for a more expensive service than provided) and unbundling (separately billing for services that should be combined) are common errors that can inflate your bill.
- Negotiate and seek assistance: If you spot an error or if the bill seems unmanageable, contact the billing department to negotiate. Patient advocates can also assist in reviewing bills and negotiating costs, sometimes reducing bills by 30 percent to 50 percent.

Prescription Assistance Programs

The cost of medications can be a significant burden, but several programs can help alleviate this:

- Patient assistance programs (PAPs): Many pharmaceutical companies offer free or deeply discounted prescription medications to people who meet certain income and insurance criteria—usually uninsured, underinsured, or struggling with high out-of-pocket costs. This is best for folks on expensive brand-name or specialty meds. For example, the PAN Foundation has provided approximately one million underinsured patients with financial aid totaling $3 billion since 2004.
- Pharmacy discount cards: Programs like GoodRx and NeedyMeds allow you to compare prices and get discounts at local pharmacies, sometimes offering better prices than insurance copays.
- State pharmaceutical assistance programs (SPAPs): State government programs (not every state has one, sadly) that help residents pay for prescription drugs, especially when costs aren't fully covered by Medicare Part D. Some programs also help with premiums or deductible costs. You apply through your state health department. Eligibility is based on income and age/disability status. Some states have disease-specific programs (e.g., for HIV/AIDS, cancer).

Financial Assistance Programs

When insurance falls short, several programs can help relieve some of the financial burden:

- Medicaid: A joint federal and state program providing health coverage to low-income individuals. Eligibility requirements vary by state, but it can be a crucial lifeline for those who qualify. As of 2024, Medicaid provided free health insurance to 81 million low-income and disabled people in the United States.

- Medicare's Extra Help Program (also called Low-Income Subsidy or LIS): Assists Medicare beneficiaries with prescription drug costs, covering aspects like premiums, deductibles, and copays. This program can save eligible individuals up to $5,000 annually on prescription drug expenses.

Shop Around for Medical Services

Don't assume that medical services have a fixed price. Costs can vary significantly between providers:

- Compare prices: Before scheduling a procedure, call different providers to compare prices. For example, by researching and choosing a different facility for an MRI, you could save hundreds of dollars.
- Self-pay rates: If you don't have insurance (or even if you do but have a high deductible), you can often ask for a self-pay or cash-pay discount. Many clinics and hospitals offer lower rates to patients paying out of pocket because it saves them the hassle of billing insurance.
- Pro tip: Don't be afraid to ask. You can ask something like, "I'm paying out of pocket. What's your best rate?" or "Do you have a self-pay discount?" In some cases, the self-pay rate can be hundreds of dollars less than the insurance-negotiated price. Don't assume the sticker price is the final price.

Advocacy and Support Networks

Beyond financial programs, support networks can offer valuable guidance:

- Patient advocates: Professionals who can help you navigate the healthcare system, understand your bills, and find financial assistance programs.
- Support groups: Connecting with others facing similar challenges can provide emotional support and practical advice on managing healthcare expenses.
- Patient Advocate Foundation (PAF): This organization offers various programs, including co-pay relief and disease-specific funds, to help with expenses like co-pays, premiums, and other out-of-pocket costs.

For more in-depth tips and strategies on navigating the complex healthcare system, consider reading *How to Be a Badass in a Broken Healthcare System* by Yours Truly. Shameless plug. This resource offers a comprehensive guide to taking control of your healthcare journey without sacrificing your financial well-being.

Another book to check out: *APPROVED: Win Your Insurance Appeal in 5 Days* by Laurie Todd. I can't tell you it is an entertaining read, but it is eye-opening. It certainly helped me change how I approach appeals.

By proactively seeking out assistance programs, meticulously reviewing medical bills, and leveraging available resources, you can alleviate some of the financial weight of medical expenses. Remember, while the maze may be complex, resources are available to help you find a way through without compromising your financial goals.

How did everyone do with this chapter? Popping the antihistamines? I hope you're feeling more confident and rash-free!

Work-Life Playbook

Résumé Highlights

- Portfolio careers (aka patchwork paychecks) are often the most flexible and sustainable path for spoonies.
- Financial skills are learned, not inherited. You don't need to be a spreadsheet sorcerer to get smarter with your money.
- Medical bills are suspect until proven accurate. Itemize everything and never assume the number they give you is the one you owe.
- Creativity can pay actual bills. You don't have to be a "real artist" or an "expert" to monetize your talents or test a side hustle.

Power Moves

- Review your last three medical bills. Request itemized statements and compare them to your insurance's EOBs. Challenge anything sketchy.
- Create a *bare bones* budget based on your *lowest* earning month—not your best. It'll cushion the slow seasons.
- Audit your recurring subscriptions and ditch anything you forgot you had. (RIP that mystery streaming service you signed up for during the pandemic.)
- Research one funding program (like your state's VR services or an SBA grant) and jot down the steps to apply—don't wait until you're desperate.

CEO Mindset Check-In

- Where could I be more creative or scrappy with my income this year?
- What do I *actually* need to spend money on to keep my work and body functioning well?
- Am I undervaluing my skills, time, or energy? If so, what would charging more look like?
- What's one financial system (budgeting, bill review, savings, etc) I could build to reduce stress later?
- Am I giving myself permission to pivot financially when my health demands it—or am I stuck chasing consistency at any cost?

Chapter 12

Survive Self-Sabotage

It was one of those high-honor, full-uniform funerals for a former police chief, with officers standing stiffly at attention beside the casket. People came to pay their respects, and the family sat in the front row.

Officer Nenia was working the detail. She was twenty-three years old and a handful of years into a law enforcement career she loved. She had big goals—the first female sergeant, then police chief in her modest community. She was already the only female SWAT operator in her state. She had just started to feel like she was hitting her stride.

And then her body handcuffed her.

Twenty minutes into the hour-long funeral shift, standing at attention, her vision blurred. The room tilted. The familiar wave of pre-syncope rolled over her. She tried to will it away. *Just hold on a little longer*, she thought. She was searching for a solution right before everything went black.

She collapsed into a candle and nearly set the casket's flag on fire.

I burst out laughing as she finished the story, and I instantly felt bad for laughing at such a serious situation. However, then I realized she was laughing, too.

"I laugh about it now, but it was mortifying at the time," she said.

No one knew Nenia had POTS. She hadn't told anyone. She didn't want to look weak in this very tough career. To this point, her Ehlers-Danlos Syndrome and POTS symptoms were mostly mild. She'd been managing them quietly by rocking back and forth during interviews, which seemed to keep her upright. Her poor chief of police suffered from motion sickness while watching her body camera footage. Welcome to spoonie life, Chief!

It wasn't until she got COVID, and eventually long COVID, that everything changed.

"It completely detonated my system," she told me. "I went from managing my health while still doing my job, to passing out after standing for three and a half minutes. My old life just wasn't an option anymore."

The uniform was handed in and the police cruiser exchanged for a wheelchair. No retirement party as she planned. Just an ending. No accommodations, no pivots, no easing out. Just done.

Nenia grieved the career she'd spent a decade building. But eventually, she turned to a hidden passion she hoped would be her retirement gig: editing. She had earned her MFA in creative writing on the side, which turned out to be very proactive. The only problem? She hadn't planned on launching a freelance career in the middle of a health crisis.

"It was supposed to be a side hustle. A future thing. Suddenly, it was my *only* thing."

And like many of us launching something new, she encountered the usual wall of invisible tasks and financial fears. I found myself nodding my head as she talked about starting her editing business.

"I couldn't work a regular nine-to-five, and definitely not one that required commuting. But building my own business? That was terrifying in a different way."

It wasn't the editing that scared her. It was the money.

Yes, adjusting to client-based paychecks rather than bi-weekly paychecks was undoubtedly at the top of her list of worries and fears, but charging what she was worth felt impossible at first. She'd spend hours researching rates, reviewing the Editorial Freelancers Association's guidelines, and prepping quotes.

"I'd be totally ready to quote the price, and then right before I hit send, I'd knock $500 off. Every single time. I was doing it to myself. I felt guilty asking for money like I hadn't earned it."

And then came the ultimate test: a sixteen-year-old potential client who surprised her during a video consultation.

"He was incredibly professional—had written a whole book, and his parents were buying him editing services for his birthday. But when I saw his face, I almost couldn't do it. I thought, *The universe is testing me right now.*"

I told her I would have caved faster than a beagle holding out for a bone. She did offer a small discount, but she didn't completely fold.

"It was a turning point. I realized I was letting guilt run my business. And that wasn't sustainable."

She credited her husband with helping her through the mental shifts. "At one point, he said, 'You're giving your work away. If you're going to volunteer your services, that's fine, but then don't pretend you're running a business.'"

It was a line she never forgot. And I don't think I will either.

As her business grew, so did her confidence and the awareness of just how precious her time and energy had become. At first, she did everything herself—built her website, learned tech tools the hard way, lost brain cells trying to figure out taxes, and refused to pay for help.

"I would spend two days watching YouTube tutorials to save a hundred dollars. It was ridiculous. Eventually, I realized my time was worth more than that."

Now, if she gets stuck on something? She hires someone. "If I can't figure it out in five minutes, I outsource it. I'm not wasting energy I don't have."

That clarity—on time, value, and what it means to work on your own terms and without guilt. It is something she built one tough lesson at a time. Nenia sets clear deadlines with built-in buffers, explains to clients that she has a health condition without oversharing, and even has a backup editor lined up in case she ever lands herself in the hospital. "That hasn't happened yet, but I want my clients to feel safe. I want to feel safe."

For her, success no longer looks like a badge, a title, or a weekly paycheck. It looks like control. Flexibility. Saved energy to spend with family. A schedule that doesn't start until 11:00 a.m. and Mondays with no meetings to recover from life.

She also utilized her past to level up her present, which I think is so badass. She leans on her police background to specialize in editing thrillers and mystery novels. It adds value for her clients and lets her bring a unique perspective to the table. It is proof that even seemingly unrelated careers can cross-pollinate in cool, profitable ways.

"I love what I do, and I can still show up for my family. I get to stop when I need to. That's what success looks like now."

How to Overcome Imposter Syndrome

Even when Nenia knew what others were charging, and that by comparison her rates were too low, she struggled to quote the full price. I felt this in my bones as I listened to her talk about it.

"I would feel so guilty asking them for money, like I was stealing from them or something." That's classic imposter syndrome—feeling like your work isn't worth what others are happily charging, even when it objectively is.

For my anchor job, I haven't increased my rates in three years. So, while my rates are now much more competitive than they used to be, I still struggle with thinking I'm not worth the dollar sign. Like Nenia, I tend to downplay skill or experience. She said she felt like she couldn't justify her rates because "I haven't been doing this long enough," or "what can I really bring to them?" Despite having an MFA and a law enforcement background that made her *uniquely* qualified to edit thrillers, as well as rave reviews from clients, she still second-guessed her value. And I totally get it.

Imposter syndrome can be a sledgehammer to your business's foundation. Let's learn how to recognize it and squash it.

What Imposter Syndrome Sounds Like

- "I know I should charge $500, but that feels like too much. I'll just cut it in half."

- "I'm not really an expert. Someone's going to figure out I have no clue what I'm doing."
- "I don't have enough certifications/clients/testimonials/energy to charge more."
- "They're just being nice. They don't really think I did a good job."
- "Who am I to be doing this?"

If any of those hit a little too hard, congrats—imposter syndrome has weaseled its way into your life. It's loud, annoying, and utterly full of crap.

Why It's So Dangerous

- It steals your income. You undercharge or overdeliver because you feel unworthy.
- It devalues your time. You dedicate hard-worked hours at a lower rate.
- It keeps your business small. You turn down big opportunities out of fear you'll be "exposed."
- It leads to burnout. You hustle twice as hard to prove your worth. And really, you're proving your worth to just yourself at that point.
- It makes you a people-pleaser, not a CEO. You start acting like you're doing favors instead of offering a valuable service.

How to Shut It Down

1. Keep a "Brag File." Save screenshots of kind client feedback, glowing testimonials, "nailed it" moments, and anything else that proves you're not a fraud. On days when you feel like a walking scam, open that file. You're not making this up.

2. Charge based on value, not guilt. Repeat after me: "I'm not selling hours. I'm selling outcomes." The person who pays you $1,000 for editing isn't buying your time; they're buying success for their important project. They're buying precious happiness. Don't discount your impact just because it only took you six hours.

3. Learn the industry standard, and stand by it. Research what others in your field are charging for their services. If your rates are wildly under that, imposter syndrome is likely robbing you blind. Let the industry numbers anchor you.

4. Don't call yourself "new" forever. Everyone starts somewhere. But if you've completed five projects, attended two trainings, and received positive feedback? You're no longer a newbie. You're there! Own it.

5. Practice saying your rate like it's your name. Not: "Um, I usually charge $300, but like, I'm open to negotiation."

Try: "My rate for that is $300." And then stop talking. Easier said than done, but practice makes perfect. Don't rush to justify or discount. Let the silence do the heavy lifting.

6. Set your schedule and stick to it. Overworking to "prove yourself" is a fast track to burnout. You're allowed to work limited hours. You're allowed to take breaks. You're allowed to need recovery time and still be a valuable hire.

7. Know that your chronic illness doesn't disqualify you. In fact, it might be your superpower. You probably work harder, plan smarter, and have more resilience than most people on your block. That's not a liability; in fact, it sounds like a strength to me!

Let Go of Comparisons and Expectations

Some days, I'd scroll through Instagram while sipping too-hot coffee (seriously, does anyone else with Sjogren's feel like *everything* is too hot?) and waiting for my meds to kick in, only to get emotionally body-slammed by someone's perfectly curated post. You know the ones: "How I made $30K in three days with zero ads, while raising alpacas, and writing a memoir!" Or my personal favorite, some watercolor pet portrait artist casually dropping their latest commission that looks like it should be hanging in a museum. Meanwhile, I'm over here second-guessing why I ever dared to pick up a brush.

It stings. And not because I'm not proud of what I do, but because comparison is a sneaky thing. It slides into your noggin and whispers, *You should be further along. You should be better at this. You'll never be as good as that.*

This is emotional sabotage disguised as self-reflection.

Social media makes this harder, especially for folks like me who *work* in social media. I spend a stupid amount of hours immersed in everyone else's wins. I see authors with massive followings building gorgeous content strategies. Creators going viral with hilarious skits. Brilliant copywriters making me think, "Why didn't I think of that?"

And then I look at my to-do list and completely second-guess my ability.

That's the comparison trap. It's the quickest way to forget your progress and invalidate your path.

We can't forget about the other side of the coin: expectations. Not the ones you've chosen, but the ones placed upon you and society as a whole. The ones you accepted as a rule of thumb until chronic illness came along. Expectations around what a career should look like, what defines hard work, or the prestige of titles.

I still kick around the idea of applying for a "real" job in patient advocacy. You know, with a hospital badge and a title that sounds impressive at family reunions. Or I think about taking a fancy agency job just to prove I can. These are the echoes of old expectations, the ones I had before my body rerouted like a historically wrong GPS.

Before I fell ill in 2019, I had a more traditional career path in mind. Promotions. 401k. Insurance and an HSA plan. My life now? It's different. Not bad, just different.

Letting go of those old expectations wasn't easy. There's grief in that process. A quiet mourning for the version of you that once existed. But there's also power in realizing that success doesn't have to look like a corner office or a six-figure launch or a LinkedIn profile full of corporate buzzwords.

Let's reframe this.

What if progress isn't measured by *achievement*, but *alignment*? What if it's not about how much you earn, but how much energy you still have after work to enjoy your life? What if the biggest win isn't scaling your business but reclaiming your health one slow morning at a time?

Hold on to your underpants, because here's a radical idea: maybe your small wins are actually huge.

Like turning down a client because your gut said no. Or raising your rates and not immediately panicking. Or giving yourself a full rest day without needing to "earn it" first. Maybe the way you measure success now has less to do with hustle and more to do with harmony. And never comparing (or at least resisting most of the time).

Here's another trick I've learned when comparison rears its jealous little head: use it as a compass. If someone's post makes your stomach flip in a "wish that were me" kind of way—pause and ask: *Is this envy or information?*

Sometimes that twinge of jealousy is really a breadcrumb. It's pointing you toward something you want. Maybe it's a creative project, a type of work, or a lifestyle that feels more aligned with your values. Don't ignore that nudge. Follow it. Let it inspire action, not shame.

So the next time you catch yourself spiraling because someone else posted a picture-perfect productivity reel, take a breath. Remember what you're building. Remember that what works for someone else might not work for you.

Let the dream evolve. Let the timeline breathe. Let go of what you thought your career was supposed to look like and build what serves you now.

And for the love of spoons, unfollow the people who make you feel like crap online. We don't have space for all that!

You're doing great. Even on the days it doesn't feel like it.

Work-Life Playbook

Résumé Highlights

- Pivoting doesn't necessarily mean starting from scratch. It may mean reworking what you already know into something more sustainable.
- Imposter syndrome is sneaky and sabotages your pricing, energy, and growth. Name it, and then shut it down.
- Guilt has no place in a business strategy. You don't owe anyone a discount on your time, talent, or labor.
- Outsourcing isn't lazy. It's a strategy. Time and energy are currencies.

- Success can look like control, freedom, and still having energy to enjoy your family.

Power Moves

- Create a pricing script and practice saying it out loud without apology or offering discounting.
- Make a "Brag File" of testimonials, wins, and moments of impact. Keep it where you can see it.
- Is there one task you can consider outsourcing to free your mind up for other tasks?
- Create a baseline schedule with built-in buffer time.
- Revisit your skills from previous careers. What can cross over into your new career? Get creative and don't overthink it.

CEO Mindset Check-In

- Where is guilt showing up for you right now? Where do you feel that guilt is coming from, and what is one step you can take today to start letting that go?
- What's one boundary you could set today that would protect your energy and sustainability?
- What part of your old career could add unique value to your current or future work?
- If you weren't trying to live up to anyone else's expectations, what would success look like for you?

Chapter 13

Build a Support System

Career success doesn't happen in a vacuum, and when you're working with a body that has its own unpredictable agenda, you can't afford to go it alone. Whether you're starting a new job, running your own business, or just trying to stay employed without running yourself into the ground, the people you surround yourself with matter. Some will push you forward, while others will make you question why you ever tried. Some will support you unconditionally, while others will insist on making your life harder than it already is. The trick is figuring out the difference and knowing how to build a support system that boosts you like a salt packet to a POTS patient.

Mentors, allies, and even the occasional well-intentioned skeptic all play a role in shaping your career, but when you're managing chronic illness, you need to be especially careful about who gets a seat at your table. Not everyone who offers advice understands what it's like to live in a body that rarely cooperates. Most traditional career mentors will have an "it's all about the grind" mentality. If you take advice from people who have never heard of the spoon theory, you're setting yourself up for frustration, guilt, and exhaustion.

A good mentor is someone who tells you the truth, even when you don't want to hear it, while acknowledging the reality you live in. I'm blessed to have plenty of mentors in my life, but only a handful have really understood the balance between motivation and sustainability. One of them was fellow author and entrepreneur Pete Smith, who had a no-nonsense approach that could be both inspiring and mildly infuriating. I invite you to check out his book, *Dare to Matter: Choosing an Unstuck and Unapologetic Life of Significance*. When I stalled on writing my first attempt at this book, he didn't let me off the hook. Instead, he hit me with, "So, are the first two chapters of your book going to be 'How to Not Write a Book' and 'How to Bullshit Yourself'?"

Ouch. But also, fair. A great mentor will call you on your crap, not to shame you but to help light a spark that you can fan into a bright flame. The right kind of support takes the form of practical, actionable advice from people who understand both your ambition and your limitations. If you don't already have someone like that in your corner, start looking. There are people out there who have walked this road before you, who know what it's like to juggle work and health, who understand that some days you're capable of taking on the world and other days just answering an email feels like a Herculean task. Those are the people you need to connect with.

You may think allies are simply people who always agree with you. Nah. They're the ones who challenge you in ways that make you better, even if it doesn't always feel like support in the moment. I used to think my husband was like wet cement in my entrepreneurial journey. I wanted to sprint to my end goal, and he was slowing me down. Every time I talked about quitting my job to start my own business, he bombarded me with a million questions. How would I handle inconsistent income? What if I lost all my clients? Did I have three months of savings in case things went sideways? How will I have health insurance? At the time, it felt really freaking discouraging. I wanted blind enthusiasm, man! I wanted someone to cheer me on no matter what, but instead, I got nonstop reality checks. And I hated it.

Reflecting back, he wasn't unsupportive. He was making sure I had a *plan*. He wasn't doubting me; he was trying to protect me from the very real financial risks that come with self-employment. I didn't appreciate it at the time, but years later, when my business hit its first rough patch and I lost half my clients overnight (thanks a lot, COVID), I realized how right he had been. If I hadn't saved up that financial cushion, then I would have been riddled with panic and guilt. Or if I hadn't factored in marketplace health insurance in my monthly expenses when I set my income goals, then I would have felt foolish and guilty. That's a tough combo. Allies may not always make you feel good in the moment, but the good ones make sure you're prepared for what's ahead.

Then there are the people who, whether intentionally or not, seem hellbent on making everything more complicated. They're the ones who drain your energy, plant doubt in your mind, or subtly undermine your progress. Sometimes they're easy to spot, like the coworker who constantly points out your mistakes while conveniently ignoring their own. Sometimes they're more insidious, like the friend who always seems to have a passive-aggressive comment about your career choices. And sometimes, they disguise pure insult and digs as constructive criticism.

Years ago, when I was working in marketing, I had a coworker who made it her mission to make my life miserable. She'd been at the company forever and had a reputation for bullying new employees. I was warned about her on my first day, but I thought my new colleagues were exaggerating. Sadly, they were not. She had a talent for drawing you into conversation just to cut you down. My work was constantly under scrutiny, and at one point, she even went to my manager and suggested that I take a graphic design course at the local community college. And as a bonus insult, she insisted on going with me. Fun times. I may have or may not have been increasing my alcohol consumption during these months.

What she didn't know was that I had spent years studying fine arts before moving into marketing. I showed up to that class with my sketchbook, sat next to her, and slowly (with a smirk) flipped through page after page of intricate drawings before finding a blank page for notes. She saw my work, stammered, and didn't say a word about my design skills again. Some people will always try to make you doubt yourself, but the only way they win is if you let them.

Not all obstacles are external, are they? Some of the biggest villains in our careers are...well, us. It's that voice in your head that tells you you're not good enough, not qualified enough, or not capable of making this work. Sometimes, we're our own worst enemies, convincing ourselves that failure is inevitable before we even start. I see it all the time—people who say they want to start a business or change careers, but instead of taking action, they get stuck in a cycle of hesitation.

I once had a professor explain how even positive change can trigger negative reactions. He told a story about a woman who started getting fit, gaining confidence, and making positive changes in her life—only to have her husband start resenting her for it. "I liked her the way she was," said the husband. I related to it instantly. Change, even when it's for the better, can make people uncomfortable. It forces them to confront things they may not be ready to deal with, whether it's their own insecurities or the fear of the unknown. I was so caught up in the story that I blurted out, "Yes! My husband still puts his meat in front of my face and expects me to eat it!" The room fell silent, and my professor stared at me with red creeping into his cheeks. I immediately wished I could disappear. You see, I had recently become a vegan, but I was the only one in the room with that information. Classic.

Change is about what you do and about how people around you react. Sometimes their discomfort can hold you back. Let's dig a little deeper and build an action plan for mentors, allies, and villains.

Find and Work With Mentors Who Sincerely Get It

Finding the right mentor when you have a chronic illness can feel like trying to find a gluten-free, dairy-free, low-FODMAP dessert that actually tastes good—technically possible, but way harder than it should be. The working world isn't exactly designed with us in mind, so traditional career mentors may not get what it's like to navigate jobs with a rebellious body. For us, this means knowing where to look, how to approach them, and how to make the most of the relationship.

Like healthcare providers, not all mentors are created equal. Some are great for helping you build a network, sharpen specific skills, or help navigate career moves, but if they don't understand the unique challenges of working while sick, they might end up pushing you toward strategies that fall flat and burn you out. A solid mentor for someone with a chronic illness should have at least one (or ideally more) of the following qualities:

- They understand flexibility. They don't push the traditional "grind until you collapse" mindset and instead help you build a sustainable career strategy.
- They respect your health limitations. They don't roll their eyes when you mention needing breaks or accommodations.
- They have industry knowledge because you need someone who can help you grow in your field.
- They offer honest, constructive feedback. A mentor's job isn't to shower you with praise or tell you what you want to hear. They should challenge you, but not in a way that ignores your reality.
- They have been in your shoes or, at the very least, helped others who have been on a similar path.

Where to Find Mentors

Chronic illness can be isolating, which makes finding a mentor even harder. But fear not, my Sweatpant Sommelier, there are plenty of places to look:

Industry and Business Support Groups

- Trade associations. Every industry has at least one trade association. They offer mentorship programs, networking

events, and education. Some even have disability-focused
initiatives.

- Small business development centers (SBDC). If you're
self-employed or thinking about it, SBDCs (funded by the
SBA) offer free mentoring, business planning, and strategy
sessions.

- Women's business centers. If you're a woman entrepreneur
or professional, these centers offer mentorship, funding
opportunities, and training.

- Chambers of commerce. Many local chapters offer
programs specifically designed for small business owners,
freelancers, or professionals seeking to grow their businesses.

Education-Based Mentorship

- Professors and college career centers. Even if you're long
past your college years, many professors love helping
former students. And career centers sometimes offer alumni
support programs.

- Workshops and online courses. The best way to find
mentors naturally is to be in the same space with people
who share your goals. Many instructors love helping
motivated students. My online patient advocacy program
at the University of Miami was a fantastic source of peers
and a professor who was more than willing to brainstorm,
encourage, and validate my feelings.

- Apprenticeship and fellowship programs. Certain industries
offer mentorship-based programs that pair you with an
experienced pro.

Social Media and Online Communities

- LinkedIn groups. Search for industry-specific groups or those focused on professionals with disabilities. Many organizations offer mentorship programs and networking opportunities.
- Facebook groups. There are thousands of groups for chronic illness professionals, freelancers, and entrepreneurs.
- Reddit & Discord communities. Subreddits like r/disabledworkers or r/freelance have people actively looking to mentor others.
- Bluesky & Instagram networking. Engaging with industry professionals and thought leaders in your field can lead to unexpected mentorship opportunities.

How to Approach a Mentor (Without Being Weird About It)

So you've found someone who seems like they could be a great mentor! Now what? You don't just DM them, "Will you be my mentor?" because that's a one-way ticket to Awkwardville. Instead, start by building a connection first.

- Engage with their work. If they write articles, post on social media, or run a business, then comment, share, or start a conversation about their insights.
- Ask a specific question. Something like: "I saw your post about breaking into [industry]. I'm trying to pivot careers while managing health challenges, and I'd love to hear your favorite tip on where to start."
- Make it clear why you're reaching out. People are busy. If you're asking for mentorship, be upfront, but keep it casual:

"I really admire your work in [field] and would love the chance to learn a few tips from you. Would you be open to a quick chat sometime?"

- Start small. Don't go straight for "Can you guide me for the next five years?" Instead, ask for a one-time conversation and see how it flows.

How to Get the Most Out of a Mentorship

Finding a mentor is only half the battle. The real work is making sure you benefit from the relationship. Too many people connect with mentors and then do nothing with the advice they get. Here's how to make sure you're not wasting their time or yours.

- Come prepared. Before meetings, have a list of questions or topics you want to discuss. Don't just show up expecting them to magically solve your career problems.
- Take action. If they give you advice, try it. Mentors don't want to keep repeating themselves if you're not taking their suggestions seriously.
- Respect their time. If they're giving you free guidance, don't treat them like a 24/7 on-call consultant.
- Be honest about what you need. If you're struggling with work-life integration or accommodations, let them know what kind of support you need.
- Give back when you can. Maybe you can't return the favor to them, but you can pay it forward by mentoring someone else down the road.

What If You Can't Find a Mentor?

Not everyone finds the perfect mentor, and that's okay. If you're struggling to connect with someone, become your own best mentor. Read books and articles from people in your field. Join online communities where people share their career wins and mistakes. Watch YouTube videos in bed. Learn from others, even if it's from a distance. A mentor can help guide you, but at the end of the day, you're the one in charge of building a career that works for you.

Look for the Right Allies

The people around you can either make your life easier or ten times harder. Allies are those rare, wonderful humans who understand that you're not lazy, not faking, and not making excuses. They see your potential and support your goals, even if those goals look different from the traditional definition of success.

The problem? Not everyone in your life is automatically an ally. Some people will mean well but offer the wrong kind of support. Others will actively make your life more difficult, sometimes without even realizing it. And sometimes the biggest obstacle is our own guilt or hesitation about asking for help.

Allies don't need to have the perfect words or even a full understanding of what you're going through. But they believe you, support you, and respect your career choices, even if they don't fully get your experience.

A good ally is someone who:

- Respects your limitations without making you feel like a burden.
- Encourages you without pressuring you to do more than you can handle.
- Listens when you need to vent instead of offering a five-step solution you didn't ask for.
- Recognizes that working while sick is twice the effort for half the credit.
- Helps in practical ways, whether that's sending you a job lead, proofreading your resume, or just reminding you that you're doing enough.

The key to an ally relationship is mutual respect. They don't treat you like a fragile doll, but they also don't dismiss your challenges. They help where they can and understand that sometimes, just having someone in your corner is enough.

Where to Find Badass Allies

Chronic illness can be isolating, especially when your energy is limited. But remember, you don't need a massive circle of allies—just a couple good ones. Here's where to start looking:

Personal Allies

These are your family members, your partner, and friends who "get it," or at least try to. I'm sure I don't have to tell you, but not all personal friends and relatives automatically qualify as allies. It's okay to redefine relationships based on who supports you in a way that helps.

- Start with the people who consistently check in. Even if they don't fully understand what you're going through, if they're showing up, they're trying.
- Look for people who don't get defensive or make you feel guilty when you set boundaries. If someone respects your need for rest, flexibility, or lower-energy activities, they're an ally.
- Don't waste time convincing skeptics. If someone repeatedly questions your illness or makes you feel guilty for not "pushing through," they're not an ally. In fact, they may belong in the "villain" section.

Professional Allies

Finding people who understand the challenges of your work is just as important as finding personal support. Whether they're a flexible boss, supportive coworker, or someone in your industry who shares similar experiences, work allies help you navigate professional settings.

- Find coworkers who operate with empathy and prioritize healthy work rhythms. Even without opening up about your health, you can usually tell who collaborates well and who's focused only on corporate climbing.
- Look for bosses who prioritize results over rigid schedules. A good manager is someone who measures you by what you accomplish, not how many hours you log.
- Connect with others who work differently. If you're freelance or self-employed, networking with other remote workers, consultants, or business owners can help you find like-minded people who don't subscribe to hustle culture.

Chronic Illness & Disability Communities

Sometimes, the best allies are the people who are walking the same path. These communities are full of people who understand what it's like to build a career while managing health challenges.

- Facebook groups, Smart Patients & Reddit communities. Look for groups focused on chronic illness professionals, disability in the workplace, or remote work with health conditions.
- Local or virtual support groups. Some advocacy organizations offer career-focused support groups for professionals with disabilities and those with chronic illnesses.
- Online platforms like The Mighty or Chronically Capable cater to disabled workers, providing networking, job listings, and community support.

How to Communicate What You Need (Without Feeling Like a Burden)

One of the hardest things about chronic illness is feeling that you have to justify your needs to people. But we often must do that, because people aren't mind readers. Even the most well-intentioned allies won't always know what kind of support you require unless you tell them.

If you're struggling to ask for help or communicate your needs, here's a simple way to frame it:

Clear Ask Formula:

1. State what you need – Be direct and specific. "I need help with..." or "It would really help me if..."

2. Explain why it matters – Give a short reason so they understand the impact.

3. Set expectations – Let them know what you are (or aren't) asking for.

Example:

Bad Ask to a Partner: "Ugh, I'm so overwhelmed with work. I don't know how I'm going to keep up. You need to help me more around the house."

Better Ask: "Hey, I've got a lot on my plate this week, and my energy is really low. Could you take the lead on the dishes and laundry this week? It will really help me knock this presentation out of the park and impress my client."

Bad Ask to a Friend: "I hate job searching. It's so exhausting. Can you go online for me and look around?"

Better Ask: "I'm struggling with the job search, and the screen time is really bothering my eyes. If you see any remote job listings that seem like a fit for me, could you send them my way?"

The more specific and actionable your request, the easier it is for an ally to step in and help.

Recognize and Deal With the Villains in Your Career

Not everyone in your career journey will be a supportive ally. Some people will actively make your life harder, whether it's through dismissiveness, sabotage, or just a general lack of respect for your limitations. And sometimes, the biggest villain in your career isn't another person at all—it's *you*. The way you talk to yourself, the fears you let hold you back, and the guilt you carry for not working like a "normal" person can be just as destructive as a toxic boss or a judgmental coworker.

Villains, whether external or internal, can slow you down, drain your energy, and doubt your potential. But like in every good story, villains only have power if you let them. The key is learning how to recognize them, shut them down, and reclaim your career without falling into their traps.

Some villains are easy to spot. The boss who refuses to approve accommodations because "everyone gets tired sometimes." The coworker who makes passive-aggressive comments about your sick days. The friend who constantly questions whether you're really that sick because she saw you at a bookstore last month. These are the obvious ones, the people who either don't believe in your illness or just don't care how it affects you. They see flexibility as special treatment and view anything outside of their own experience as an excuse. They can make work unbearable and drain what little energy you have left.

The biggest mistake you can make with these villains is assuming they'll figure it out on their own (you know, like you did with your diagnosis). They won't. You have to set boundaries, correct assumptions, and be clear about what you can and can't do. If a boss or coworker doesn't take your health needs seriously, document everything and don't hesitate to bring in HR or legal protections. If a friend keeps pushing unrealistic job opportunities, tell them, "I appreciate the thought, but that type of work isn't possible for me right now. Here's what I'm looking for..." If a client ignores your work hours, reinforce them by saying, "Thanks for reaching out! I'll take a look and get back to you during my next work window."

Shutting Them Down: Comebacks for When People Say the Wrong Thing

People love to give unsolicited opinions about careers, especially when they don't understand what it's like to work while chronically ill. You're bound to hear some deeply frustrating, wildly inappropriate, or just plain clueless comments.

Please remember that you don't always have to engage! Sometimes, the best response is to ignore and conserve your energy. But if you're in the mood to shut it down, here are some snappy yet professional ways to respond.

When a Boss or Coworker Downplays Your Health Needs

"Everyone gets tired."
"That's true, but fatigue due to a disease process is on a whole other playing field."

"You don't look sick."
"And you don't look like a doctor."

"You're so lucky you get to work from home."
"Yes, I appreciate being able to control my work environment, and I'd trade that 'luxury' in a heartbeat for a body that didn't make it a requirement though."

"Can't you just push through?"
"Sure, and then we can discuss who's covering for me when I inevitably crash and have to miss even more work."

"I wish I could take that much time off."
"I wish I didn't have to. You can borrow my chronic illness for a week - I'd love to take time off from that."

"I've worked with people who had [insert random illness] and they never needed accommodations."
"That's great for them. Everyone's health journey is different."

When Someone Judges Your Career Change or Job Flexibility

"Why would you leave a stable job?"
"Because 'stable' doesn't mean 'healthy.' My goal is to have a job and sustain my health, not impress LinkedIn."

"You should just stick it out."
"Stick what out, exactly? The slow erosion of my health? The chronic stress? I think I'll pass."

"You'll regret giving up a traditional job."
"I'd regret giving up my health and sanity even more."

"Isn't that kind of a step down?"
"You mean a step toward a life that doesn't wreck me? Feels like a step up."

"But don't you want to keep climbing the ladder?"
"I'd rather build a ladder that fits my life instead of breaking my back trying to climb one that wasn't built for me."

"That's not a real job."
"It pays my bills, respects my health, and provides fulfillment. Sounds pretty real to me."

When Someone Questions Your Work Ethic

"Must be nice to work fewer hours."
"Must be nice to have a body that doesn't malfunction daily."

"Are you sure you're not just overthinking this?"
"Are you sure you're not under-thinking it?"

"I don't think it's that hard."
"Then I invite you to live in my body for a week and get back to me."

"I worked full-time while dealing with [insert unrelated struggle]."
"That's great, but health challenges aren't a competition. I'm focused on what works for me."

When Someone Offers Unsolicited Advice

"Have you tried yoga?"
"No, but I've tried patience, and it's running out."

Or if you want a reply with less snark:
"My health issues are a bit more complex than that, which is why I work closely with my physicians."

"Maybe if you changed your diet, you wouldn't need accommodations."

"And maybe if I had a different body, we wouldn't be having this conversation."

"You should just think positively."
"Oh, my bad! Let me just manifest my way to a fully functional immune system."

When Friends or Family are Discouraging

For this group, I want to be clear: Not everyone deserves an answer or reply. You don't owe that jealous friend an explanation for your career changes. You can simply say, "None-ya…none-ya business."

"Working for yourself sounds way too risky. Stick with a traditional job for the benefits."
"I understand your concerns, and I had them as well. I have conducted extensive research and carefully weighed the pros and cons of a more traditional job. I have made an informed decision on what is best for me at this time."
Note: This answer will vary greatly depending on who you are talking to. For example, your partner or parent (depending on your age) has a right to know how you are saving money for tough times or how you'll handle health insurance. But Susan down the street doesn't need to know the details of your situation.

"We would all like to work from home part-time, but that just isn't reality."
"Yes, there is a lot of appeal to working from home and making your own hours, and it also comes with tremendous hard work, sacrifice, and planning for it to be successful…or everyone would do it."

"When are you going back to a real job?"
"It sounds like you are referring to societal norms of a 9-5 job. That is no longer the reality of today's workforce, and I'm proud of the very real work that I do."

"What do you even do all day?"
"It depends on the day, which is why I created a flexible career. Some days I am [insert humble brag] and other days I may be managing symptoms or doctor's appointments."

"There's no job security in freelancing/gig life."
"Lay-offs or getting fired are possible in traditional jobs as well, especially when you are chronically ill. I have taken necessary steps to provide financial stability should I encounter a loss of income."

Some days, you won't have the energy to respond. And that's okay. Not every villain needs to be fought. But on the days you feel like reminding people that you're not here to justify your existence, these responses should help.

But keep in mind that some villains can't be fixed. If a job, boss, or work culture is repeatedly making you sick, it's okay to walk away. Your health is more important than a paycheck. And if that sentence makes you panic because you can't afford to quit? That's even more reason to start quietly planning your exit strategy.

Recognize the Villian in the Mirror

As frustrating as external villains can be, sometimes the most dangerous one is the voice inside your own head. Chronic illness can make you your own worst enemy without you even realizing it. The voice that tells you you're not doing enough. The guilt that creeps in every time you have to rest instead of work. The fear that keeps you from applying for a better job or charging what you're worth, because what if you can't keep up?

This villain is tricky because it disguises itself as responsibility, ambition, or humility. It tells you that slowing down means giving up, that setting boundaries means being difficult, that resting means slacking. It's the one whispering, "Maybe you're not sick enough to need accommodations," or "Other people are working harder than you." It's relentless, and if you don't fight back, it will keep you stuck in cycles of burnout, self-doubt, and unnecessary suffering.

The only way to defeat this villain is to change the way you talk to yourself. Would you tell a friend with your exact health issues that they're lazy for needing breaks? Would you tell them they don't deserve a flexible job or fair pay? No, you would not. Then why is it okay to say those things to yourself? Start replacing those thoughts with truth:

"I'm doing the best I can with the energy I have."

"Rest is a necessity, not a luxury."

"I am allowed to build a career that works for me, not against me."

It takes practice, but the more you challenge those thoughts, the less power they have over you.

Villains thrive in silence and self-doubt. The more you tolerate toxic behavior, the more they will take from you. The more you let self-criticism run unchecked, the more it will sabotage your success.

The key to building a sustainable career while managing chronic illness is knowing who belongs in your inner circle. Find the mentors who push you forward without pushing you over the edge. Find the allies who uplift and listen to you. Distance yourself from the people who drain your energy, even if they mean well. And most importantly, learn how to recognize when you're being your own worst enemy.

You don't have to do this alone, but you do have to be intentional about who you let in. Surround yourself with people who understand what you're working toward, who respect the limitations you have, and who remind you that success is about building something sustainable.

Work-Life Playbook

Résumé Highlights

- The people you surround yourself with can either support your success or drain your energy, so choose wisely.
- A good mentor pushes you forward without pushing you over the edge. They challenge you but respect your reality.
- Allies aren't just people who agree with you. Allies are the ones who show up when it counts, even if their support doesn't always look the way you expect.
- Some people will subtly undermine your success under the guise of support. Recognizing these "stealth villains" is just as important as spotting obvious ones.
- Your biggest career villain might be you (gasp!). Fear, self-doubt, and internalized guilt can sabotage you just as much as a toxic boss or coworker.
- The strongest career move you'll ever make isn't forcing yourself to fit into a broken system—it's creating a work life that allows you to thrive.

Power Moves

- Identify the key people in your work life. Who are your mentors, allies, and potential villains? Write down their names and determine who is genuinely helping versus who is holding you back.
- Find a mentor who understands the challenges of flexible work or living with a chronic illness. Start with trade associations, LinkedIn, someone already in your network, or industry support groups.
- Practice setting clear boundaries with work relationships. If a coworker, boss, or client consistently drains you, rehearse and use one of the comeback lines from this chapter.
- Build your ally network. If you don't have supportive colleagues or friends in your corner, consider joining a new professional group or a chronic illness network, or find even just one person who understands your work challenges.
- If you've been tolerating a toxic work situation, decide on a first step to change it. Whether it's standing up to a difficult boss, adjusting your workload, or setting clear expectations with a client, take one small action to shift the power dynamic in your favor.

CEO Mindset Check-In

- Do you have a mentor who truly understands flexible work, sustainable success, or the challenges of chronic illness? If not, where can you start looking?
- Have you been tolerating a toxic work environment or relationship because you feel like you have no other option? What would it take to change that?

- What internal dialogue or belief about work is holding you back? If a friend were in your shoes, what would you tell them?
- If you could design your ideal work setup without fear or judgment, what would it look like? What's one step you can take toward making that a reality?
- What's one career decision you're avoiding because of fear, self-doubt, or guilt? What's the worst that could happen if you took a step forward?

Chapter 14

Flare-Friendly Career Ideas

Depending on your needs and interests, there are several different ways to start building a list of job possibilities to consider and research. For example, we can examine the ease of acquiring new skills, popularity, or industry-specific trends. This is by no means a comprehensive list, but it is certainly enough to spark your entrepreneurial spirit.

The goal in looking through this list is to allow for exploration without "buts." For example, if you read "photography" and your soul jumps for joy, but your brain says, "But you cannot physically tolerate that job," I want you to just put that "but" on the shelf for now. It may eventually be a no, but you owe yourself a moment to brainstorm possible accommodations and solutions that would allow you to take on that job.

Circle, highlight, or write down the ones that immediately get you curious or excited when you read them.

Admin and Operations

Virtual Assistant
What You'll Do: Support clients with admin tasks like inbox management, calendar scheduling, and social media updates.
Skills Needed: Organization, communication, Google Workspace.
Why It's Spoonie-Friendly: Highly flexible and customizable workload and hours.

Operations Coordinator
What You'll Do: Manage workflows, project logistics, and cross-team coordination.
Skills Needed: Project management tools, time management, and communication.
Why It's Spoonie-Friendly: Structure-based role with options for remote, paced work.

Transcriptionist
What You'll Do: Convert audio or video recordings into written text.
Skills Needed: Typing, listening, grammar, and accuracy.
Why It's Spoonie-Friendly: Solo, quiet work with flexible deadlines.

Online Moderator
What You'll Do: Oversee online communities, review content, and enforce guidelines.
Skills Needed: Judgment, communication, and internet literacy.

Why It's Spoonie-Friendly: Asynchronous and low-physical-impact work.

Resume or LinkedIn Profile Writer

What You'll Do: Help clients craft compelling resumes and online professional profiles.
Skills Needed: Writing, editing, ATS knowledge, and branding experience.
Why It's Spoonie-Friendly: Independent, deadline-driven, and brain-fog adaptable.

Consulting and Coaching

Career Coach

What You'll Do: Guide individuals through career transitions, resume planning, or interview prep.
Skills Needed: Coaching, empathy, and a strategic mind.
Why It's Spoonie-Friendly: Self-scheduled and built around client flexibility.

Business Consultant

What You'll Do: Advise small businesses on growth strategies, structure, or operations.
Skills Needed: Business planning, communication, Excel, or planning tools.
Why It's Spoonie-Friendly: Project-based and goal-oriented for flexible delivery.

Creative Coach

What You'll Do: Support clients in overcoming creative blocks or launching artistic goals.

Skills Needed: Encouragement, planning, and excellent communication.
Why It's Spoonie-Friendly: Energy-adaptable sessions with no strict time tracking.

Chronic Illness Coach

What You'll Do: Help others living with chronic illness plan sustainable routines and manage limitations.
Skills Needed: Empathy, organization, healthcare knowledge, and peer experience.
Why It's Spoonie-Friendly: Deeply aligned with your energy, mission-driven, and flexible.

Creative and Content

Freelance Writer or Copywriter

What You'll Do: Write blog posts, emails, social media captions, or long-form content for clients.
Skills Needed: Writing, grammar, and audience awareness.
Why It's Spoonie-Friendly: Flexible deadlines and remote access let you work when you're able.

Graphic Designer

What You'll Do: Design logos, brand assets, marketing materials, or social media graphics.
Skills Needed: Design tools like Adobe Creative Suite or Canva, branding, and marketing.
Why It's Spoonie-Friendly: Creative, project-based work that can be done at your own pace from home.

Video Editor

What You'll Do: Edit video content for YouTube, marketing campaigns, educators, or short-form social media use.

Skills Needed: Video editing software, storytelling, timing, and file management.

Why It's Spoonie-Friendly: Allows for independent work on flexible timelines, often with few live meetings.

Illustrator or Digital Artist

What You'll Do: Create custom illustrations or digital art for products, print, or content platforms.

Skills Needed: Procreate, Adobe Illustrator, drawing tablets, and digital creativity.

Why It's Spoonie-Friendly: Work solo with creative control and project-based pacing.

Voiceover Artist

What You'll Do: Narrate audiobooks, training videos, ads, or educational content from a home setup.

Skills Needed: Clear voice, audio editing, and microphone use.

Why It's Spoonie-Friendly: Flexible deadlines and remote work from your own recording setup.

Photographer or Photo Editor

What You'll Do: Take or edit photos for products, portraits, events, real estate, or social media campaigns.

Skills Needed: DSLR or smartphone camera use, Lightroom, and Photoshop.

Why It's Spoonie-Friendly: Editing work can be done remotely and flexibly around flare days.

Etsy Digital Downloads Creator

What You'll Do: Design digital products like planners, templates, checklists, or coloring pages.

Skills Needed: Canva, Adobe, or similar tools, creativity, and customer service.

Why It's Spoonie-Friendly: Passive income once set up; work in short bursts or batch on good days.

Customer and Community Support

Customer Support Representative

What You'll Do: Answer customer questions and resolve issues via phone, email, or chat.

Skills Needed: Patience, writing, and software like Zendesk.

Why It's Spoonie-Friendly: Low barrier to entry, remote, and often scheduled in blocks.

Tech Support Specialist

What You'll Do: Troubleshoot tech problems for software, hardware, or app users.

Skills Needed: Tech knowledge, communication, and product familiarity.

Why It's Spoonie-Friendly: Often remote with training and part-time options.

Community Manager

What You'll Do: Foster engagement and safety in online communities (like social media) or forums.

Skills Needed: Content moderation, excellent communication skills (especially writing skills), and social media tools.

Why It's Spoonie-Friendly: Generally built around an agreed-upon response schedule (Ex, Check Facebook page and DMs every 3-4 hours during weekdays).

Chat-Based Customer Support

What You'll Do: Provide customer service solely through chat—no phone calls.

Skills Needed: Clear and quick typing, multitasking, and the ability to learn a support platform.

Why It's Spoonie-Friendly: Lower sensory demand and easier on the voice, good for those with auditory or speech limitations.

Online Focus Group Participant / Survey Taker

What You'll Do: Participate in paid studies, usability tests, or market research. An example is Rare Patients, but always read the fine print of how they use your information. Engage at your own risk.

Skills Needed: None required beyond honesty and clarity.

Why It's Spoonie-Friendly: Totally flexible, low commitment, and low stress.

Health and Wellness

Health or Wellness Coach

What You'll Do: Support clients in making sustainable lifestyle and health-related changes.

Skills Needed: Coaching skills, knowledge in a specific health area, empathy, and planning tools.

Why It's Spoonie-Friendly: Set your own hours and pace around client sessions.

Yoga or Meditation Instructor

What You'll Do: Lead group or private classes virtually or in person for stress and mobility support.

Skills Needed: Instruction, movement knowledge, and mindfulness techniques.

Why It's Spoonie-Friendly: Sessions can be short, calm, and scheduled when you feel best.

Nutrition Consultant

What You'll Do: Advise clients on meal plans or dietary adjustments.

Skills Needed: Nutrition/dietitian knowledge, communication, and ability to execute customization.

Why It's Spoonie-Friendly: Remote-friendly and often scheduled around your chosen availability.

Patient Advocate

What You'll Do: Help individuals understand medical options, navigate insurance, and access care.

Skills Needed: Research, excellent written and verbal communication, and healthcare literacy.

Why It's Spoonie-Friendly: Flexible caseload and remote-friendly workflow.

Education and Research

Online Tutor

What You'll Do: Teach students in a specific subject over video sessions.

Skills Needed: Subject expertise, patience, and teaching ability.

Why It's Spoonie-Friendly: Schedule directly with students around your best times.

Curriculum Developer

What You'll Do: Create educational materials and lesson plans for classrooms or e-learning platforms.

Skills Needed: Instructional design, subject knowledge, and formatting.

Why It's Spoonie-Friendly: Independent, creative, and deadline-based.

Research Assistant

What You'll Do: Collect, organize, and analyze data for academic or private sector studies.

Skills Needed: Research skills, Excel, and citation formatting

Why It's Spoonie-Friendly: Often asynchronous and adaptable to mental energy windows.

Entrepreneurial Ventures

E-commerce Store Owner

What You'll Do: Sell handmade or print-on-demand goods via platforms like Etsy or Shopify.

Skills Needed: Product creation, creating marketable listings, and customer service.

Why It's Spoonie-Friendly: Run your own schedule and scale based on your capacity.

Blogger or Content Creator

What You'll Do: Write or film content in a niche and monetize via ads, sponsors, or products.

Skills Needed: SEO, storytelling, video tools or blogging platforms.
Why It's Spoonie-Friendly: Creative, flexible, and can be batch-produced around symptoms.

Dropshipping Business Operator

What You'll Do: Manage an online store by sourcing products shipped directly from suppliers.
Skills Needed: E-commerce platforms, marketing, and customer service.
Why It's Spoonie-Friendly: No physical inventory, low-lift systems, and scalable.

Online Product Reviewer

What You'll Do: Test and review products for sellers or brands on e-commerce platforms.
Skills Needed: Analytical, honesty, and excellent written communication.
Why It's Spoonie-Friendly: Review at your pace, no calls or video required.

Finance and Business Services

Accountant

What You'll Do: Manage finances, reconcile books, and prepare taxes for businesses or individuals.
Skills Needed: At least a bachelor's degree in accounting or a related field like finance or business. To become a certified public accountant (CPA) (the top credential), you'll need 150 college credits (often a master's degree) and to pass the CPA exam. Also bookkeeping software and spreadsheets.

Why It's Spoonie-Friendly: Remote-friendly, often seasonal or project-based.

Financial Consultant

What You'll Do: Help clients with budgeting, investment strategies, or retirement planning.

Skills Needed: A bachelor's degree in finance, accounting, economics, or a related business field. Achieving professional certifications like the certified financial planner (CFP) or chartered financial analyst (CFA) significantly boosts credibility client. You'll also need communication skills and reporting tools.

Why It's Spoonie-Friendly: Meeting-based and adaptable to preferred hours.

Technology and Development

Web Developer

What You'll Do: Build and maintain websites for clients or organizations using code or platforms.

Skills Needed: HTML, CSS, JavaScript, and WordPress (or similar).

Why It's Spoonie-Friendly: Project-based, remote-friendly work with solo focus options.

App Developer

What You'll Do: Develop custom mobile apps for iOS and Android devices.

Skills Needed: Swift, Kotlin, Flutter, React Native, and API integration.

Why It's Spoonie-Friendly: Coding can be done in bursts during energy highs and around your schedule.

AI/ML Engineer

What You'll Do: Design, test, and improve machine learning models and algorithms.

Skills Needed: Python, TensorFlow, PyTorch, statistics, and data analysis.

Why It's Spoonie-Friendly: Deep focus work that can often be done remotely and asynchronously.

Data Analyst

What You'll Do: Analyze trends, create reports, and provide insights from datasets.

Skills Needed: Excel, SQL, Power BI, and data visualization.

Why It's Spoonie-Friendly: Work can be scheduled during brain-sharp hours and done remotely.

Cybersecurity Specialist

What You'll Do: Identify security vulnerabilities, monitor threats, and protect digital systems.

Skills Needed: Network security, encryption, AI, firewalls, and ethical hacking.

Why It's Spoonie-Friendly: High pay potential and remote contracts available with project-focused timelines.

Blockchain Engineer

What You'll Do: Develop and test blockchain applications, smart contracts, and protocols.

Skills Needed: Solidity, Rust, blockchain frameworks, and cryptography.

Why It's Spoonie-Friendly: Remote-first industry with flexible timelines and asynchronous communication.

Cloud Computing Engineer

What You'll Do: Manage cloud infrastructure, build serverless apps, and support deployment.

Skills Needed: AWS, Azure, Google Cloud, and DevOps tools.

Why It's Spoonie-Friendly: Most roles are remote and allow for pacing work around fatigue levels.

Marketing and Online Growth

Social Media Manager

What You'll Do: Schedule posts, manage engagement, and analyze performance for brands or individuals.

Skills Needed: Platform knowledge, Canva, video editing, analytics tools, and self-driven to stay on top of best practices and trends.

Why It's Spoonie-Friendly: Offers flexibility in scheduling content and working in energy bursts.

Digital Marketing Consultant

What You'll Do: Plan and execute campaigns across email, ads, and websites to improve traffic and sales.

Skills Needed: Email tools, Google Ads, analytics, and CRM software.

Why It's Spoonie-Friendly: Can work remotely, asynchronously, and in a project-based flow.

Content Strategist

What You'll Do: Develop plans for content creation, publishing, and SEO alignment.

Skills Needed: Editorial planning, SEO, and audience research.

Why It's Spoonie-Friendly: Often remote and focused on deliverables, not hours clocked.

Affiliate Marketer

What You'll Do: Promote products using personalized links to earn commissions.

Skills Needed: Marketing, blogging, social sharing, and SEO.

Why It's Spoonie-Friendly: Self-paced, passive-income potential, and location-independent.

Online Course Creator

What You'll Do: Design and sell educational content in your area of expertise.

Skills Needed: LMS platforms, presentation tools, and video creation.

Why It's Spoonie-Friendly: Content can be batch-created when energy allows, then sold passively.

Rare, Wacky, and Hidden Gems

This list is where the quirky meets chronic. These roles aren't always posted on big job boards, so they may be difficult to find, but they exist. Whether you're channeling vibes, narrating ambiance, or getting paid to sit in Zoom calls, these hidden gems offer neat ways to earn money on your terms.

Audio Describer for the Visually Impaired

What You'll Do: Narrate or write descriptions of nonverbal elements in films, TV, or live performances.

Skills Needed: Descriptive writing, timing, script formatting, and attention to detail.

Why It's Spoonie-Friendly: Work is often freelance, creative, and done remotely with solo focus.

Pet Psychic or Tarot Reader (Virtual)

What You'll Do: Offer intuitive or spiritual readings for pets or people via email, video, or livestream.

Skills Needed: Intuition, card reading, communication, and storytelling.

Why It's Spoonie-Friendly: Entirely schedule- and energy-controlled with highly personalized client pacing.

Greeting Card Writer

What You'll Do: Write short, funny, sweet, or clever messages for greeting card companies or Etsy shops.

Skills Needed: Humor, emotional intelligence, and copywriting.

Why It's Spoonie-Friendly: Very short-form work that can be completed in batches when brain energy is high.

Naming Consultant (for Brands, Books, Babies, etc.)

What You'll Do: Brainstorm and pitch name ideas for products, startups, pets, or humans.

Skills Needed: Wordplay, creativity, market awareness, and linguistic insight.

Why It's Spoonie-Friendly: Work is conceptual and solo with no physical demands and minimal deadlines.

Fake Wedding Guest or Professional Mourner (Virtual or In Real Life).

What You'll Do: Attend virtual or in-person events to make numbers or fill social roles. While it hasn't gained in popularity in the U.S., it is a very real gig in other countries.

Skills Needed: Emotional expression, discretion, and basic video etiquette (for virtual roles).

Why It's Spoonie-Friendly: Quirky and brief gigs with rest time before and after built in.

Color Consultant (Digital or Interior)

What You'll Do: Help people select color palettes for home design, branding, or personal style.

Skills Needed: Design sense, trend knowledge, and color theory.

Why It's Spoonie-Friendly: Advising roles can be virtual and done during creative windows, not fixed hours.

Etsy Spell Jar Seller or Digital Witchy Shop Owner

What You'll Do: Create digital or physical witchy products like intention jars, spell kits, or rituals.

Skills Needed: Crafting, design, spirituality knowledge, and packaging (for physical items).

Why It's Spoonie-Friendly: Work can be batched and sold passively with creative freedom.

Remote Jury Focus Group Participant

What You'll Do: Watch mock trials or case summaries and give feedback to help lawyers prepare.

Skills Needed: Listening, analysis, and feedback articulation.

Why It's Spoonie-Friendly: Paid opinion sharing with no ongoing obligation and 100 percent virtual.

Background Actor for Virtual Events

What You'll Do: Sit quietly in Zoom meetings or webinars to fill out a crowd or audience.

Skills Needed: None beyond showing up, muting, and nodding occasionally.

Why It's Spoonie-Friendly: Literally just sit still and get paid— ideal for rest days.

Digital Stickers or Planner Template Designer

What You'll Do: Create downloadable stickers, templates, or trackers for digital planning apps.

Skills Needed: Canva or Adobe, attention to aesthetics, and layout.

Why It's Spoonie-Friendly: Batch design on good days, then sell passively with minimal upkeep.

Niche Audio Creator (e.g., fantasy tavern ambience or stormy background noise)

What You'll Do: Produce looping audio tracks for writers, gamers, or ASMR fans.

Skills Needed: Basic sound editing, creativity, and ambient layering.

Why It's Spoonie-Friendly: Creative and quiet work with lots of flexibility and automation options.

Human Sound Tester

What You'll Do: Listen to audio files and rate them for clarity, tone, or emotional accuracy.

Skills Needed: Listening skills, attention to nuance, and basic rating input.

Why It's Spoonie-Friendly: Often short assignments, perfect for low-energy or reclined working.

Remote Mystery Shopper (Chat or Email Based)

What You'll Do: Pose as a customer to test online service quality, especially via chat or email.

Skills Needed: Writing, curiosity, and observation.

Why It's Spoonie-Friendly: No phone calls or meetings required, and you control the pace.

Work-Life Playbook

Résumé Highlights

- There are so many more options than just 9-to-5 office jobs—don't let outdated thinking box you in.
- "Work you love" and "work you can do with chronic illness" are not mutually exclusive.
- You don't need to be 100 percent symptom-free to pursue meaningful, flexible, and financially sustainable work.
- Some jobs you can grow into slowly. Others you can batch when you feel good. The goal is options, not pressure.

Power Moves

- Circle or highlight every job that even slightly sparks interest even if you have doubts. No "buts" yet.
- Pick three from your "yes" list and research what real-life people say about the work on Reddit, YouTube, or blogs.

- Take one option and brainstorm what an "accommodated" version might look like for you. (Shorter hours? Voice tools? Adjustable deadlines?)
- Use Notion, a spreadsheet, or pen and paper to sort your "maybes" by energy required, income potential, or training needed.
- Check sites like Skillshare, Coursera, or even social media to learn more about skills needed without overcommitting.

CEO Mindset Check-In

- What kind of work tasks make you feel good (even if you're pooped)?
- What environment helps you work best—solo, quiet, collaborative, fast-paced?
- Are you looking for income right now, creative fulfillment, long-term potential…or all three?
- What flare-day realities do you need to build around (fatigue, mobility, brain fog, pain)?
- What would a "win" look like for you in a new job? More income? More autonomy? Less stress?

Chapter 15

Defeat the Health Insurance Monster

Insurance is gross. Is it gross that insurance can help people afford their healthcare? No, that's definitely not the ick part. What is gross is the bloated, bureaucratic, greedy mess that is the American health insurance system. The hours spent on hold. The denial letters that feel like they were written by a robot with a grudge. The premiums that cost nearly as much as your rent, paired with deductibles so high you'd need a GoFundMe to use the damn insurance you're paying for.

And yet, here we are. But just because it's gross doesn't mean we get to opt out. If you're living with a chronic condition, health insurance can be a lifeline. Understanding how to choose the right plan, use it wisely, and overcome challenges when it fails absolutely has a direct impact on your new career venture.

This chapter is to help you avoid the landmines, keep more money in your pocket, and reduce insurance industry defeat. You deserve a system that doesn't make you cry into your claims paperwork, and the best way to stop those tears is with knowledge.

I've had all types of insurance over the years. I've had no insurance, marketplace insurance, employer-sponsored insurance, or my spouse's insurance. I can tell you, from personal experience, which was the scariest for me (no insurance) and which was the most fabulous (my employer-based insurance). Paying out of pocket is fabulous until it isn't. When that ER visit or high-ticket drug or test comes along, then it's bye-bye savings and hello panic town. The spoonie reality check is that the consequences are high for the chronically ill and disabled. Therefore, we aren't going to dive into that option.

Truthfully, I had a dang difficult time writing this chapter because the health insurance world is constantly changing. Inevitably, this information will likely be outdated a month after this book is published. Please do your own research or consult an insurance broker before making any major decisions.

Choose the Right Plan Without Crying Into Your Keyboard

Figuring out health insurance can feel so overwhelming, but under no circumstances can you skip this step in creating your new career roadmap. Whether you are looking into an employer's plan, a marketplace plan, or a med-sharing plan, asking some straightforward questions before you start comparing options is a solid place to start.

Five Key Questions to Ask Before Choosing a Plan

1. "Will this plan cover the specialists I need?"
Listen, I would do mildly illegal things to keep my unicorn providers. For spoonies, our care team matters a whole heck of a lot. When I was considering getting on my spouse's insurance,

I called my rheumatologist's office and his insurance company three times each to ensure I got the same answer: "Yes, this insurance is accepted by this provider and considered in-network." Always check before committing, because we worked damn hard to build a trusted care team, so losing someone on that team comes with a high price.

2. "What's the real out-of-pocket cost (beyond the monthly premium)?"

When I left my traditional job and bought insurance from the marketplace, I only considered the monthly cost. Boy, did that come back and bite me later. $95 copays add up quickly when you have health issues. Add up the deductible, copays, coinsurance, and out-of-pocket max to get the whole picture.

3. "How does this plan handle my medications?"

Two of my medications have to be brand-name, and they come with the same horrible side effect: they are nauseatingly expensive. Check the insurance company's formulary list (the plan's covered drugs). Are your prescriptions included? Are they subject to step therapy or prior authorization? How much will you have to pay for a non-formulary drug?

4. "What hoops will I have to jump through for approvals?"

Some plans require prior authorization or referrals for expensive meds, MRIs, or specialist visits. Fewer hoops usually mean fewer headaches, but they typically come with a higher price tag. Is it a nightmare to get a referral from your PCP, or are they usually helpful with those hurdles? If not, consider a PPO plan that allows you to move about the system more independently.

Although keep in mind that many specialist offices require a referral, even if your insurance plan does not.

5. "What happens if my health takes a left turn (again)?"
Look at the plan's out-of-network coverage, emergency care policies, and yearly out-of-pocket maximum. Spoonies need flexibility for unpredictable care needs.

When making calls to offices and insurance companies, record the representative's name, date, and confirmed answer (read it back to them to ensure you heard them correctly). Receipts matter.

Lower Deductibles Versus Lower Premiums

We must understand the core trade-off between lower premiums and lower deductible plans. Premiums are like your monthly Netflix subscription. Whether you watch one show or fifty, you pay the same flat subscription. In comparison, deductibles are like buying movie tickets on top of Netflix when your favorite shows aren't included. Premiums keep the lights on, but deductibles are the price of admission before insurance starts covering the popcorn.

Five Key Factors to Consider for Spoonies

1. How often do you need healthcare?
If your calendar is filled with specialist appointments, infusions, imaging, labs—or you take high-cost meds frequently—plans with lower deductibles and higher premiums usually save you money in the long run. As Prudential puts it, "Low deductibles are best when an illness or injury requires extensive medical care."

However, if you're stable, in maintenance, or enjoying remission (cheers!), and your doctor visits and prescription needs are minimal, a higher-deductible plan with lower premiums may be a more budget-friendly choice.

Ultimately, it's about anticipating your care needs and picking the plan that offers the sweetest trade-off between what's predictable and what saves you overall.

2. What are your prescription costs?

This one is often overlooked, but medications usually eat up your budget faster than we burn through ibuprofen. Please keep in mind that some plans don't apply prescriptions to the deductible, which means you benefit from low copays even on high-deductible plans. That's a huge win if you depend on meds every month. You just need to make sure that you check the plan's formulary list to confirm that your drug is covered, see what tier it's in (which affects cost), and determine whether you'll need prior authorization.

If you rely on specialty meds or biologics, a lower deductible plan or one with strong drug coverage may be worth the higher monthly premium. That choice could be the difference between sticking to your treatment and rationing doses—or worse, skipping them altogether. Been there. Not fun. Research shows that even moderate increases in copays can reduce medication adherence and increase hospitalization risk.

3. What is the out-of-pocket maximum (OOP max)?

This is your hidden safety net, because once you hit this limit, the plan must cover 100 percent of your healthcare for the rest of the year. This is where the math gets imperative, because a lower OOP max, even with higher premiums, may save you thousands if you're a frequent waiting room flyer.

4. Consider your cash flow vs. predictability.

What may seem like the cheapest sticker price may not be as sustainable as you think. Thank God for calculators, because we have to lean hard into math here!

Lower Deductible Plan: You pay more monthly, but your expenses are spread out and more predictable.

Higher Deductible Plan: You save monthly, but a single flare or ER visit could leave you suddenly owing thousands.

Head to your bank account, or if you are one of those annoyingly organized people who save medical receipts (I lash out because I'm insecure about my organizational skills), look back at the last couple of years to see your medical cost averages by copays, ER visits, and medications. You may have better or worse years ahead, but this will give you a baseline of sorts.

5. Don't forget the priceless bits.

For those providers you trust or the hospital you demand to be taken to in an emergency, keeping them covered by your insurance can be priceless. Lower-premium plans (often HMOs or EPOs) may restrict your provider network. If you need access to specialists at specific hospitals, then the savings from lower premiums may backfire if your providers are out-of-network.

Real-Life Scenarios: How Premiums and Deductibles Play Out

I'm a visual learner, so let's see what this may look like in real life (through totally fake people). Here are two examples that show how your healthcare usage can change, and which plan saves you money.

Scenario 1: Taylor—high medical needs

Taylor pays a $600 monthly premium (a level that's pretty average for Silver-tier ACA plans in 2025) and faces a $5,000 annual deductible. With multiple specialists and biologic medications costing thousands monthly, Taylor hits the deductible within just a couple of months. From that point on, insurance kicks in heavily. Taylor would likely save more over the year with a higher premium, lower deductible plan—a trade-off that brings predictability and financial relief.

- Premium: $600/month ($7,200/year)
- Deductible: $5,000
- Healthcare Usage: Experts estimate that biologic medications can run $5,000+/month, plus specialist visits and labs.

Taylor is likely to hit that $5,000 deductible within the first couple of months, after which most of the rest of the year's care will be covered. For someone in Taylor's situation, choosing a higher-premium plan with a lower deductible offers better budget predictability and lower total annual costs.

Scenario 2: Sam—low medical needs

Sam rarely visits the doctors and takes low-cost prescriptions. Sam chooses a more affordable $400 monthly premium plan with a $7,000 deductible. Because Sam has low healthcare needs, he never reaches the deductible. The result? Sam pays much less overall throughout the year.

- Premium: $400/month ($4,800/year)
- Deductible: $7,000

Sam's out-of-pocket costs remain consistently low, with minimal usage; Sam doesn't reach the deductible, meaning the lower-premium plan ultimately saves money overall.

If brain fog makes this a miserable task, consider reaching out to a friend or family member for help. You can get free help from ACA Navigators found at healthcare.gov.

Insurance Alphabet Soup—WTF Do All These Plans Mean?

Decoding health insurance plan types feels like trying to read upside-down Roman numerals with a migraine, but knowing the difference between an HMO and a PPO is important for you and your bank account. Here's your spoon-sized breakdown:

HMO (Health Maintenance Organization)

Think of an HMO as an exclusive club. You can only see the doctors in your network, and you need a referral from your primary care provider (PCP) to see any specialist. It's cheaper in terms of monthly premiums and copays, but you give up a lot of flexibility.

Translation: If you're okay playing "Mother, may I?" with your PCP and don't mind sticking to the insurance-approved crew, this might be a budget-friendly choice.

PPO (Preferred Provider Organization)

A PPO is like VIP access to almost any doctor you want. No referral needed (unless the clinic or hospital requires it), and you can go out-of-network (though it may cost more).

Translation: You're paying more for the privilege of freedom. If you're managing complex or rare health issues and need specialist access on your terms, this might be worth the extra cash.

EPO (Exclusive Provider Organization)

EPOs are a hybrid of HMO and PPO. You don't need a referral to see specialists, but only if they're in-network. Out-of-network care? You're usually footing the whole bill.

Translation: Slightly more freedom than an HMO, but still very much "don't step outside the bubble."

POS (Point of Service)

You pick a PCP and need referrals like with an HMO, but you can go out-of-network if you're willing to pay more (and jump through more hoops).

Translation: It's the indecisive sandwich of insurance plans— some HMO rules, some PPO flexibility, but with a side of paperwork.

HDHP (High Deductible Health Plan)

This plan is low on monthly premiums but high on the amount you have to pay before insurance kicks in. Often paired with a health savings account (HSA).

Translation: You're paying less upfront but must shell out more cash before your coverage actually starts doing anything useful.

HSA (Health Savings Account)

This is your insurance piggy bank. You can stash money here tax-free to cover qualified medical expenses. It's only available if you have a high-deductible plan.

Translation: This is one of the few helpful things insurance companies offer, so if you're eligible, take advantage of it.

FSA (Flexible Spending Account)

An employer-based account where you set aside pre-tax dollars to pay for qualified medical expenses like copays, prescriptions, and over-the-counter necessities. But if you don't use it, you lose it (except for a small rollover amount or grace period, if your plan allows).

Translation: It's like medical meal prep. Plan ahead, use it wisely, and don't let it rot in the fridge or it's gone forever.

Catastrophic Health Plans

These are ultra-low-premium plans designed for people under thirty or those who qualify for a hardship exemption. The catch? You'll pay almost everything out-of-pocket until you hit a massive deductible, and coverage is bare-bones.

Translation: Catastrophic plans are like a broken umbrella. They only help when the hurricane hits, but you'll get soaked in every regular storm.

Medicare and Medicaid Basics

Medicare: Federal insurance for people 65+ or those with qualifying disabilities. It's broken into Parts A, B, C, and D. But for spoonies, the main thing to know is to check prescription coverage and be aware of gaps. Medicare Advantage plans (Part C) work like PPOs or HMOs but can limit access to specialists.

Medicaid: A state and federal program for people with limited income or resources. It can be added support for chronic illness care since many states cover expensive treatments and medications better than marketplace plans.

Translation: Medicare is your milestone birthday gift from the government, and Medicaid may be the surprise-you-might-qualify option no one bothers to explain. Check eligibility as it could save your budget.

Short-Term Health Plans

These "affordable" plans get aggressively marketed, especially online, but beware: They're not ACA-compliant and can deny coverage for pre-existing conditions. They may look cheap up front, but surprise bills lurk behind every corner. If it were food, it would be an appetizer. Not a full meal. They are meant to fill gaps in coverage and sold by private insurers.

Translation: Short-term plans are Band-Aids. You don't want to depend on them too long.

COBRA (Consolidated Omnibus Budget Reconciliation Act)

If you lose your job, COBRA lets you keep your employer-sponsored insurance for a limited time, but you'll pay 100 percent of the premium plus a small admin fee. It's often pricey, but worth considering if you're mid-treatment, on expensive meds, or deep in pre-approvals.

Translation: COBRA can be an expensive umbrella in a storm. However, you may find more affordable options in the ACA marketplace.

Okay, hopefully you are not crossed-eyed and hanging in there with me. But if you are amped up and looking for extra credit, check out Chapter 6: How to Navigate Insurance & Financial Landmines in my previous book, *How to Be a Badass in a Broken Healthcare System*, for more cost-savings ideas.

Work-Life Playbook

Résumé Highlights

- The plan that looks cheapest up front often costs the most later—always compare total out-of-pocket costs, not just the premium.
- Spoonies must prioritize coverage that fits their *real* healthcare usage, not their most optimistic version of themselves.
- Your out-of-pocket maximum is your safety net—know it and plan around it.
- Insurance language is designed to confuse you; break it down into bite-sized parts so you can make confident decisions.

Power Moves

- Start with your five big questions. Ask whether your specialists are covered, how meds are handled, what your out-of-pocket max is, and how the plan handles emergencies and referrals.
- Compare the *real* math. Add up premiums, copays, and deductibles from your past year of care to estimate your annual spending under each plan.

- Document everything. Keep a spreadsheet or notes app with dates, names, and what each rep said. If you ever need to appeal a denial, this is gold.
- Revisit your plan annually. Health needs change, and so should your coverage. Open enrollment is your chance to realign your plan with your current reality.

CEO Mindset Check-In

- Am I choosing a plan based on hope or how I currently use healthcare?
- Which specialists, treatments, or meds would truly wreck my budget if not covered?
- What's my tolerance for unpredictability? Do I prefer stable monthly costs or flexible coverage?
- Do I understand my plan well enough to advocate confidently when claims or authorizations get messy?

Chapter 16

The Entrepreneur's Encyclopedia

Hey, fancy pants, congrats on making it this far! You've figured out what kind of work lights you up, what kind of boundaries keep your body from falling apart, and how to build a career that (mostly) respects your limitations. But here come the business logistics.

Forms. Legal jargon. Acronyms that sound like medical conditions. Stuff that makes your eyes glaze over faster than a pharmacy insert.

That's why I built this next section.

Consider this your *Entrepreneur's Encyclopedia*—a spoon-friendly, easy-to-digest rundown of the business-y things you need to know when you're freelancing, consulting, selling your own stuff, or building a career with multiple income streams. Think of it as your sidekick when the questions start creeping in, like:

- "Do I need an LLC or can I just wing it as a sole prop?"

- "Wait, what's a DBA again?"
- "Do I really have to track every business expense or just the ones that feel important?"
- "Should I open a business bank account, or is that only for people with, like, six-figure empires and letterpress business cards?"

Each section gives you:

The Quick & Dirty: a short, straight-to-the-point definition that tells you what the heck it is.

Here's the Real Deal: what you actually need to know if you're chronically ill, low on energy, juggling multiple gigs, or just trying to make smart choices without wasting spoons.

This is not meant to overwhelm you or be completed in one sitting. Skim when needed. Come back later. Use it as a tool when you're stuck or unsure. Let it sit in the back of your mind until you're ready to level up your business game.

You don't need to know everything in one panic-inducing read. You just need an understanding of what should be on your radar, and that's precisely what this little encyclopedia delivers.

Legitimizing Your Business (Without Crying...Much)

Sole Proprietor vs. LLC vs. S-Corp

Quick & Dirty: A sole proprietorship is the simplest and most common structure. It's just you, doing business under your own name. An LLC (limited liability company) is a separate legal entity that can protect your personal assets if your business ever gets sued. An S-Corp is a tax designation that can help reduce self-employment taxes once you're making a steady profit, but it's a bit more complex.

Real Deal: If you're just starting out, a sole prop may be the easiest to get up and running—no paperwork, no fees, no fuss. But if your work involves contracts, clients, or any kind of risk (think consulting, freelance creative work, coaching), you may want to form an LLC to protect your personal finances. The LLC gives your business legitimacy and separates your personal assets from those of your business. It is an important layer of protection in a sue-the-pants-off-you world. But don't stress— this is something a good accountant can walk you through (and should walk you through!).

Business Registration Requirements in Your State

Quick & Dirty: Some states require all businesses, including sole props, to register. Others only require registration if you're forming an LLC or using a trade name.

Real Deal: Go to your secretary of state's website and check what's required. It's usually not hard or expensive. Think of it as the first step in making your business official. Bonus: It can help when setting up a business bank account or applying for programs/grants designed for small businesses.

DBA (Doing Business As)

Quick & Dirty: A DBA lets you operate under a name that's not your personal legal name. For example, if your name is Susan Jones but you want to run "Flareproof Freelance," you need a DBA.

Real Deal: DBAs are useful if you want a business name that better reflects your brand or services. It also looks more professional on invoices, websites, and client contracts. You'll need to register it through your state (or sometimes your county), and the cost is usually under $100.

Banking, Bookkeeping, and Tax Stuff That You Can't Ignore

Separate Your Business and Personal Money

Quick & Dirty: Open a business checking and savings account.
Real Deal: It doesn't matter if you're only making $100 a month; you need to separate your work money from your personal money. This is crucial for legal protection and a cleaner audit trail. You'll thank yourself during tax season.

Track That Income and Expense, Babe

Quick & Dirty: Use Wave, QuickBooks, or a spreadsheet—just use *something*.
Real Deal: Monthly check-ins beat last-minute meltdowns. You don't need to track *everything* in real time, but stay consistent.

Estimated Quarterly Taxes

Quick & Dirty: If you'll owe more than $1,000 this year, you probably need to pay taxes every quarter. The IRS expects businesses to make regular payments throughout the year.
Real Deal: Use the IRS EFTPS site. And yes, this is the most annoying adult chore, but it avoids scary letters and interest fees. You will get hit with a penalty if you pay all at once at tax time.

Paycheck? Set Aside Money First!

Quick & Dirty: When you work for yourself, no one's taking taxes out of your checks, so you have to do it.

Real Deal: Every time you get paid, treat it like a gross paycheck from a job. That means 25–30 percent should be set aside for taxes before you even think about rent, groceries, or new that new guilty-pleasure book. Open a separate savings account and think of it as "TAXES—DO NOT TOUCH" and move that money immediately after each deposit. Nothing ruins a good freelance month like realizing you spent your tax money on groceries and now owe Uncle Sam.

Filing Taxes with a Chronic Illness Twist

Quick & Dirty: April 15 is tax day, extension or not. You should also make estimated quarterly tax payments to avoid penalties.

Real Deal: If you can't pay the full amount, file anyway and request a payment plan. Avoiding it just adds interest (and stress).

File Your Annual Report

Quick & Dirty: Most states require LLCs (and sometimes other business entities) to file a brief annual report and pay a minimal fee to remain in good standing.

Real Deal: This isn't a scary IRS thing. It's a state-level thing that says, "Hey, I'm still in business." You'll usually file it through your Secretary of State website. The cost is generally between $10–$500, depending on your state, so it's a "budget once a year" kind of deal. Mark your calendar because if you miss the deadline, they can dissolve your LLC (yep, even if you're still working and paying taxes). And missing the deadline usually comes with a fine.

Tell the IRS You're a Real One (Optional but Encouraged)

Quick & Dirty: Get an EIN (employer identification number).
Real Deal: It's free. It protects your Social Security number.
It makes you look more official. Use it for W-9s and business
banking.

If You Hire Someone, the IRS Wants to Know

Quick & Dirty: If you pay a freelancer or independent
contractor $600 or more in a year (this amount may vary
depending on your location and is subject to change, so always
consult with your accountant), you may be required to send
them a 1099-NEC and report it to the IRS.
Real Deal: Even if you're a freelancer yourself, if you subcontract
another person (like a virtual assistant, designer, or writer), you
officially count as a "payer." Before you send them a dime, have
them fill out a W-9 form so you have their tax info. This must
be stored securely and with great consideration. You may even
request that it be completed directly through your accountant.
Then at the end of the year, you'll send them a 1099-NEC
summarizing how much you paid them and file a copy with the
IRS. This isn't optional! This is how you stay in good standing
and avoid penalties. Thankfully, tools like QuickBooks, Wave,
or HoneyBook make sending 1099s super easy.

Deductions and Saving Smart

Home Office Deduction

Quick & Dirty: If you have a dedicated workspace at home, you
may be able to deduct it.

Real Deal: Even if it's a corner of your bedroom, it may be eligible. Just document it properly and discuss with your accountant.

Mileage & Travel

Quick & Dirty: Track mileage if you leave home for business stuff. *Real Deal:* Keep a notebook in the car or use a note app on your phone to track any meetings, errands, work trips, and other related mileage.

SEP IRAs and Retirement Planning

Quick & Dirty: You can save for retirement *and* lower your tax bill. *Real Deal:* SEP IRAs, solo 401(k)s, or Roth IRAs are great tools. You don't have to max them out—just get in the habit.

Emotional Side of Being a Boss

Accepting Variable Income

Quick & Dirty: Income fluctuates. Please remember that it's not a personal failure. You'll learn your business's trends in income and activity the longer you're in business.
Real Deal: Aim for a 3–6 month emergency fund when you can. Safety nets are a must for spoonies. Can you afford your meds and specialty appointments on top of your usual bills if you are without income for a few months?

Getting Paid Like a Professional

Quick & Dirty: Send invoices. Use contracts when appropriate. Act like a business, even if it's just you and your cat. Let's be real, your cat is probably the boss of you.

Real Deal: Confidence is contagious. If you treat your work seriously, others will, too. I once hounded a client for six months for payment. With a contract in place, you have the legal means to demand that payment (and I suggest including interest in the contract of 2-4 percent every month past due).

When to Outsource

Quick & Dirty: If it drains your energy and isn't your zone of genius, see if you can afford help.

Real Deal: Bookkeeping, tech setup, or even an assistant for invoicing can preserve your energy and sanity. List the pros and cons, including the potential cost and hours gained (which could mean more money in your wallet).

I know these tasks and responsibilities are enough to trigger a mast cell rebellion, but here is a to-do list to help push back the overwhelm. Tackle one thing at a time, and please take the time to understand what the task is, how it may apply to you, and the basics. Over time, you'll become proficient in the ways of entrepreneur life.

The Spoonie Business Launch Checklist

STEP 1: Define Your Business Basics
☐ Decide what service, product, or skill you're offering.
☐ Identify your ideal client or customer.
☐ Choose your business name (personal name or brand?).

STEP 2: Choose Your Legal Structure
☐ Decide if you're a sole proprietor, LLC, or something else.

☐ If forming an LLC, research your state's registration process.

☐ If using a name that isn't your own, file a DBA ("doing business as").

STEP 3: Make It Official

☐ Check your state's secretary of state website for registration rules.

☐ Apply for an EIN from the IRS (free and easy).

☐ File any necessary licenses or permits for your work.

☐ File your LLC's annual report (usually required every year).

STEP 4: Set Up Business Banking and Finances

☐ Open a separate business checking account.

☐ Open a savings account just for taxes.

☐ Set aside 25–30 percent of every payment you receive for taxes.

☐ Pick an accounting or bookkeeping system (even a spreadsheet works).

☐ Track all income and expenses monthly.

☐ If paying other freelancers, collect W-9s and prep for 1099-NEC forms.

STEP 5: Know Your Tax Responsibilities

☐ Learn your estimated quarterly tax deadline.

☐ Set calendar reminders for when payments are due.

☐ Save receipts for things like your home office, mileage, and subscriptions.

☐ Meet with a tax pro if you're unsure (just one call can save you future headaches).

STEP 6: Protect Your Business

☐ Create simple contracts for clients or customers.

☐ Look into business insurance if you offer services or sell goods.

☐ Add a privacy policy and terms of service to your website if needed.

☐ Use a disclaimer if your business includes advice, coaching, or education.

STEP 7: Build a System That Works for You

☐ Pick a payment/invoicing platform like PayPal, Stripe, or HoneyBook.

☐ Set up reusable templates for contracts, emails, and invoices.

☐ Define work hours and boundaries that protect your energy.

☐ Choose a tool like Trello, Notion, or ClickUp to manage tasks at your pace.

STEP 8: Revisit and Refine

☐ Re-evaluate pricing, offerings, and workload after 3–6 months.

☐ Adjust based on your health—do you need to pivot, outsource, or rest?

☐ Celebrate small wins (because showing up *is* success).

Work-Life Playbook

Résumé Highlights

- You don't need a six-figure empire to open a business bank account, track expenses, or file a DBA.

- Even spoonies are subject to the IRS's nonsense. Quarterly taxes are real. So is the satisfaction of being prepared instead of panicking when you get hit with a fine.
- Treat your work like a real business, and people will start treating you like a real business.

Power Moves

- Open a "Do Not Touch" savings account for taxes and start sliding 25–30 percent from every payment into it.
- Choose one thing to systematize this month: contracts, invoicing, or tax tracking. Make a template and save yourself spoons later.
- Apply for an EIN. It's free, fast, and keeps your Social Security number out of client paperwork.
- Audit your business banking setup. If everything's still running through your personal Venmo, it's time for an upgrade.
- If there are items you can possibly write-off, then start documenting it properly. You may end up taking a standard deduction anyway, but at least you will have everything organized and documented at the end of the year.

CEO Mindset Check-In

- What business chore have I been putting off due to fear or confusion, and how can I break it down into one manageable step?
- How can I make my business work with my flare days, not against them?

- What is draining you financially? Energetically? Make a list, then circle the items that are worth the effort. We want to keep those. For example, having three pets drains me often, but I wouldn't trade them for all the money in the world.

Conclusion

I was pacing on my porch like a new parent outside of the maternity ward. My "baby" was about to be delivered: that is, my first book. I had taken on extra work to cover the investment. I had used any extra spoons I could find to work on it. I stopped buying clothes and cancelled TV subscriptions. I made sacrifices because I found something that filled me with so much passion and purpose that I might have burst if I hadn't shared it with the world.

I had a successful business (that anchor job we discussed) that kept me busy. Fulfilled? Not really, but close enough to keep me focused and motivated. But getting sick really did teach me many valuable lessons about the healthcare system, trusting your gut, and how to listen to your body. *How to Be a Badass in a Broken Healthcare System* was not only a love letter to my sick self, but it was a hand extended to others walking the very same messed-up path as I.

When the mail truck finally approached my driveway, I stopped breathing. This was it! This was my author's proof copy of my very first book. Would the colors on the cover look great?

Would the font on the inside be readable and formatted well? I snagged the box from the letter carrier with a thanks and ran inside to see the physical evidence of my labor of love.

It was perfect (to me, anyway). I carried that book around for three days straight, checking every page. And then a new emotion crept in: *fear*. Oh my Kindle gods, people are actually going to read the words that I wrote! They're going to know personal stories—I talk about pooping, or lack of it, for Pete's sake! Are readers going to think my tips were terrific or trash? *What. Have. I. Done?*

Whether you're writing a book, starting a new job, or creating a business, there will always be moments of doubt, regret, and worry. It is totally normal. Being strategic, utilizing solid information, and practicing self-reflection are key to pushing through uncomfortable moments.

Satisfied my baby had a chance of success, I clicked "publish." And held my breath.

I cherished every positive review that rolled in. My goal going into that book was to help just one person get the answers and care they deserved. You can imagine how my heart grew as the positive Amazon reviews hit double digits and people started sending me private messages about how the book helped them. It gave me so many happy-tears moments. I want you to strive for your magic moment. Close your eyes. What does that moment look like to you? What are you hearing? What are you doing? Who is around you?

Did my book fund a vacation to Fiji? Ah, no. But it wasn't supposed to. I had built a tailored, sustainable career that paid my bills *and* fueled my dreams. I learned to appreciate my anchor job in digital marketing even more because it allowed me the ability to cross off becoming an author from my bucket list. Embracing your previous experience and skill set in a steady job helps pay for those co-pays and prescriptions. Build out from that foundation to create a patchwork of businesses, gigs, or jobs.

As you look back at your notes from the Work-Life Playbooks at the end of each chapter, I hope you make "Pause and Pivot!" your mantra. Too often, we categorize something as a failure when all it really needs is to breathe and morph into something slightly different. This book was supposed to be a rah-rah get-off-your-ass-and-become-an-entrepreneur guide. I was finally going to write and finish a manscript (this was before the *Badass* book)! I was so close to finishing it that I could smell the printed pages. Having my autoimmune system implode wasn't just a blow to my health but my dreams as well. I felt so defeated when I got sick and wrongly assumed the hard work I'd poured into the original version of this book was a waste of time. My battle with words shifted to battles in the exam room, and that was ok. It was what was needed at the time.

My illness changed my view of grit and success, and I was grateful for the re-frame. When I had the ah-ha moment of re-working my original career book into the one you're reading now, I was lit-the-freak-up. I had ideas. I had a purpose again. I had a vision board, dang it! Ok, what I really had was a slightly manic new-project energy that made me think time was a suggestion and rest was optional.

I know now that wasn't the best way to do it.

Yes, I was excited and motivated, and had a fire under my butt that probably could have powered a mid-size city. But doing everything all at once is an express lane to collapse. I was moving too fast, missing key details, making careless blunders, and burning through energy reserves I didn't have. I was trying to speedrun a marathon with a backpack full of bricks. Passion is great. Purpose is beautiful. But if you don't pace yourself, both of those things become liabilities instead of strengths.

As you start planning the next chapter of your career to leave the hustle culture behind, allow your ideas to be negotiated, rebranded, or scaled back as you experiment. Success is not synonymous with urgency. That go-go-go mentality is part of the corporate ladder we're bashing to smithereens, and we're using the scraps to build a life raft. While the traditional ladder pressures you to monetize everything, turn passion into pressure, and justify misery for a sparkly job title, the raft will help keep you afloat with stable, dependable jobs, provide work that feeds your soul, and give you the flexibility you need.

When you're starting something new—whether it's a business, a career pivot, a side hustle, or a new job—you need to give yourself permission to go one step at a time. That means picking *one* thing to focus on first, not five. That means writing everything down—all the ideas, all the goals, all the shiny "maybe someday" dreams—and then ruthlessly deciding what can wait. That means organizing your tasks not by what sounds impressive, but by what matches your current energy levels and helps satisfy your most urgent needs first. Do the high-focus work when your brain is at its sharpest. Do the mindless stuff when you feel like a zombie with Day Five Unwashed Hair. Remember, the whole point is building a career that fits your real, beautiful, complicated, chronic-life reality.

And when you hit a milestone, even a small one, please celebrate. Small wins can absolutely be sexy wins. Take a happy moment. A breath. A quiet (or loud as hell) acknowledgment that you did something hard, and you did it on your terms. Write it down. Tell a friend. Buy a cookie.

The point is to *try* to do the right things, at the right pace, in the right order for you. And to not beat yourself up if you stumble or need a break. You are building something brick by brick. Go slow, yet steady. Be scrappy *and* strategic.

Every misstep, milestone, and magical moment is rooted in learning. If you take anything away from this book, I hope it is to embrace the challenge and thrill of learning. Push through the fears and head-scratching moments, and it'll lead to accomplishments you'll be proud of for years to come. I believe in you!

Thank You!

Thank you for reading *Chronically Ill, Wildly Capable!* I hope it will help you on your journey to a life of fulfillment and sustainable accomplishments. You can find my other resources at www.littleenginepatientadvocacy.com.

Also, my heartfelt thanks to the interviewees. You made time to share your stories with me, and I'm deeply grateful. This book is better because you're in it.

Please reach out to me on social media @LittleEnginePatientAdvocacy to brag about your plans and dreams, you wildly capable creature!

About the Author

After years of being dismissed by medical providers while living with multiple unchecked autoimmune diseases, Kristina Kelly learned firsthand how difficult it can be to get timely answers and appropriate care. Drawing on her background in healthcare, she taught herself how to advocate more effectively, and eventually went back to school to become a board certified patient advocate. Through her work at Little Engine Patient Advocacy, Kristina creates practical resources designed to educate and empower fellow spoonies. She lives a quiet life with her husband, two rescue mutts, and a cat who firmly believes he's a dog. While she's deeply committed to writing practical, accessible resources for the chronic illness community, she secretly hopes to one day write a fiction book (with dragons and unicorns, of course).